"From the very first page, John Baggett draws you into a world of tragedy, faith, and hope. Masterfully intertwining both psychological and faith-based perspectives, Baggett peers into the lives of those who have struggled against all hope. Whether working through your own tragedy or seeking help for others, *Finding the Good in Grief* will bring you comfort, understanding, a sense of fortitude, and peace."

—MARGARET PATCHETT, provost, Cabarrus College, Concord, NC

"There are times when we psychiatrists find our diagnoses and evidence-based treatment responses peripheral to a patient's experience of loss. The questions of "Why me?" and "Did I deserve this?" take center stage. John Baggett's broad experience has allowed him to engage these questions of ultimate meaning in a way that would allow us to recommend him as a counselor to our patients. *Finding the Good in Grief* carries its readers forward with honesty and comfort, without flinching away from the reality of pain. It is a book that belongs on every psychiatrist's bookshelf, ready to offer at a time of such need."

—KENNETH GILBERT, psychiatrist, Champaign, IL

"A useful, readable, practical, and spiritually and psychologically balanced book about everyday faith and personal crises, written for and from the crucible of real life."

—JOHN FREER, psychiatrist, Hopkinsville, KY

"I found *Finding the Good in Grief* to be real, honest, and most of all theologically correct."

—REV. DIANE R. COX, hospital chaplain, Cary, NC

"John Baggett touches tender places. *Finding the Good in Grief* fills an important gap in addressing real issues of hurting people.... Professional and lay care providers will want to share this book with those experiencing the pain of loss and the need for support."

—REV. DAVID HILTON, retired minister and hospice chaplain, Lebanon, OH

# FINDING THE GOOD IN GRIEF

## REDISCOVER JOY
## AFTER A LIFE-CHANGING LOSS

## JOHN F. BAGGETT

Kregel
Publications

*Finding the Good in Grief: Rediscover Joy After a Life-Changing Loss*
© 2013 by John F. Baggett

Published by Kregel Publications, a division of Kregel, Inc., P.O. Box 2607, Grand Rapids, MI 49501.

The author and publisher are not engaged in rendering medical or psychological services, and this book is not intended as a guide to diagnose or treat medical or psychological problems. If medical, psychological, or other expert assistance is required, please seek the services of your own physician or certified counselor.

All Scripture quotations, unless otherwise indicated, are from the Holy Bible, New International Version®, NIV®. Copyright © 1973, 1978, 1984 by Biblica, Inc.™ Used by permission of Zondervan. All rights reserved worldwide. www.zondervan.com

Scripture quotations marked NRSV are from the New Revised Standard Version Bible, copyright © 1989 by the National Council of the Churches of Christ in the U.S.A. Used by permission. All rights reserved.

ISBN 978-0-8254-4319-0

Printed in the United States of America

# Contents

*Acknowledgments*  **7**

1  What I Feared Has Come upon Me  **9**

**STEP 1 • Trust God and Rely on Others**
2  Shock: Like Being Struck by Lightning  **19**

**STEP 2 • Choose Reality Instead of Illusion**
3  Denial: It's Not a River in Egypt  **33**
4  Escape: You Can Run but You Will Only Get Tired  **44**
5  Victimism: Where's a Superhero When You Really
   Need One?  **54**

**STEP 3 • Resist the Temptation to Get Stuck**
6  Questioning: Why Do You Keep Asking Why?  **69**
7  Anger: Who Pushed Humpty Dumpty?  **81**
8  Depression: Never Put a Period Where a Comma Belongs  **93**

**STEP 4 • Recognize Moments of Grace**
9  Acceptance: The Road to Recovery Is Paved with Moments
   of Grace  **109**

**STEP 5 • Discover New Meaning and Purpose**
10  Calling: Transform Your Season of Grieving into a Lifetime
    of Caring  **125**
11  Affirmation: When the Caterpillar Dies, the Butterfly Flies  **138**

*Epilogue*  **153**
*Notes*  **155**
*About the Author*  **157**

# ACKNOWLEDGMENTS

I have known several times of tragedy in my life. I have also experienced many moments of grace during my seasons of grieving. This book has drawn significantly on those difficult times and reflects my own journey of faith in the midst of them.

*Finding the Good in Grief: Rediscover Joy After a Life-Changing Loss* has also been inspired by the struggles of many others. I am especially indebted to the members of the National Alliance on Mental Illness (NAMI) of North Carolina who shared their personal stories with me while I was working during the 1980s on my doctoral dissertation, *Self-Stories and Coping Styles of Families with Mentally Ill Relatives.* I am grateful as well for the insights I have gained over several decades from other members of support groups, class participants, and individuals I have counseled.

The stories in the following chapters were constructed from bits and pieces of the lives of real people who have touched my life over the years. The main story lines reflect the actual life crises of specific persons, but the individual characters and narrative events used to convey the stories generally have been composed from the journeys of more than one person, with names and identifying information altered to protect anonymity. Most of the dialogue is fictional and is intended to serve the dramatic purposes of the chapters.

In bringing this book to fruition, I have been blessed with some wonderful manuscript readers: Rev. Diane Cox; Dr. Margaret Patchett; Sarah Gustafson; Diane C. Baggett; Rev. Ron De Genaro; John Freer, MD; Rev. David Hilton; Rev. Dr. Jack Good; Rev. Charles Sensel; and Kenneth Gilbert, MD. Each provided invaluable comments that have made this a much-improved book from the initial draft. In addition, my friend of many years Michael Miller, as he did during the writing of my first book, *Seeing Through the Eyes of Jesus*, once again spent many hours doing fine editing as well as providing substantive suggestions. It is difficult to imagine this final product without the assistance of each of these distinguished readers.

Finally, I wish to dedicate this book to my wonderful wife, Diane, the love of my life, who worked with me on this project every step of the way. Not only have her personal times of tragedy and moments of grace inspired insights in these pages, but she is an amazing grief counselor whose talent, training, and experience have been an invaluable resource.

JOHN F. BAGGETT
*January 2013*

# 1

# WHAT I FEARED HAS COME UPON ME

*What I feared has come upon me;*
*what I dreaded has happened to me.*
JOB 3:25

The thing you feared, the thing you hoped would never happen, has come upon you. Do you think you will ever forget where you were, what you were doing, or the way you felt at the time? Do you remember asking yourself, "Is this really happening?" Did you pray for God to make it not so? And then, as the awful truth penetrated your heart, did you cry out, "Why, God? Why did you let this happen?"

The worst thing that ever happened to me did not happen to me. It happened to my son, Mark. In his teen years, Mark was a gifted and talented young man with a bright and promising future. On many occasions he expressed the desire to do something worthwhile with his life, and he often spoke of preparing himself for a profession that would help other people and make a positive contribution to society. I shared his idealism and his dreams. But when he was seventeen, within a few weeks, everything changed.

Mark began to act strangely. He laughed at inappropriate times. He spent long hours in his room talking loudly and incoherently. He sometimes approached me with wild eyes to rant about a friend having used mental telepathy to give him a heart attack. And just when I thought things could not get any worse, they did. Mark began to have episodes of violent anger. He broke things and punched holes in the interior walls of the house. It was all bizarre and frightening. At first I did not know what to think. I suspected he might be on drugs. But I soon learned that my son had experienced the onset of schizophrenia, a brain disease that stole his personality and changed him forever. Though I did not know it at the time, the tragedy of Mark's schizophrenia would forever change me too.

After the onset of the disease, the son I had known no longer existed. In his place was another very different son, one who occasionally reminded me of the old Mark but was nothing like him most of the time. I grieved the loss of the child I had known for seventeen years. Anxiety and anguish filled me as I came to grips with the troubled soul who took his place.

Over the next few years, in response to my son's illness, I experienced at various times the stages of grief that Dr. Elizabeth Kübler-Ross identified in her book *On Death and Dying*. After the initial few days of emotional shock at the onset of Mark's illness, I underwent, as so many grieving persons do, periods of denial, anger, bargaining, and depression, along with what I believe to be other stages not identified in the Kübler-Ross model. These were not neatly defined, progressive steps in my season of grief but messily recurring moods and behaviors.

Although my grief was profoundly personal, it was not unique. To live in this world is to be touched by loss. *Grief is a universal experience.* People everywhere feel emotional pain and struggle to understand their suffering.

Furthermore, while in my grief I felt like I was on a dark and lonely journey, I was not the only one in emotional pain over the change in my son. Family and friends were also feeling the loss. *Grief is a social experience.* When a personal tragedy happens, it almost always happens to a group of people, even though it may affect some more harshly than others and even though individuals may cope with it in profoundly different ways.

*Grief is also a normal experience.* It is a mistake to believe grief can be avoided if we have enough strength of character or enough faith. When we suffer a loss, whether we are among the strong or the weak, whether our faith is small or great, we naturally experience grief, not as a sign of weakness but as a manifestation of our humanity.

*Grief is as necessary to emotional healing as physical discomfort is to bodily healing.* Without pain, for example, we likely would not protect physically injured parts of our bodies long enough for recovery to occur. Similarly, the pain of a season of grief can serve as natural protection for our emotional injuries until they have time to heal.

*The experience of grief is an integral part of life's spiritual journey.* Whether we consciously realize it or not, the stages of grief are charged with emotional and spiritual significance, reflecting not only our changing relationships with our losses but our shifting relationships with God as well.

*We have navigated the journey of grief successfully when we have reached acceptance.* Acceptance makes it possible for us to heal, to carry on with our lives, and ultimately to complete our journeys. As with physical injuries that disfigure and disable, emotional scars may last a lifetime. Nevertheless, once we have embraced and affirmed our new realities, we are able to feel emotional and spiritual peace once more.

As I struggled with my son's illness, acceptance took a long time coming. I think this was for two significant reasons. First, my emotional energy was being constantly consumed by grief as well as taxed by the daily stress of caring for a seriously disabled family member. Second, my son's illness threw me, a person of faith, into a crisis of faith.

I always had known that bad things can happen to people of faith and to those they love. But in my heart of hearts, I must have believed for a very long time that as long as I remained God's faithful minister and servant, God would put a shield of protection around my family. After all, as a young pastor I had answered God's call and moved from the familiar security of rural Tennessee to spend thirteen years in Christian ministry in three of the most challenging, crime-ridden inner-city neighborhoods of Chicago. Twice I had been caught in the cross fire between rival street gangs. My family had experienced rocks with threatening notes attached to them come crashing through our windows. We had lived through the riots that followed Martin Luther King's death, a home invasion, and the discovery of a dead body lying against our garage. Surely, I reasoned, if we had survived all of those things and if I continued in God's faithful service, then God and I had a deal: he would not let anything bad happen to me and those I love most.

The tragedy of my son's illness shattered my illusion of invincibility and laid bare the inadequacy of my naïve faith. I found myself journeying through a dark spiritual night, struggling with a new lucidity about life, and feeling overwhelmed by sadness. In the midst of my grief, my faith was tested profoundly as I struggled with an unwillingness to face and accept the reality of my son's condition.

The nineteenth-century Christian philosopher Søren Kierkegaard wrote in *The Sickness Unto Death* of the ways in which "unfaith" manifests itself at differing levels of consciousness when one is faced with life's difficulties. As I reflected on my own journey, Kierkegaard clarified for me that *the stages of grief are far more than a natural healing process; there are mortal temptations within each one.* We can make choices, whether consciously or unconsciously, that either delay healing or prevent it altogether. By making poor choices in our coping strategies and by continuing in a stage of grief when it is time to move on, we can stray from the healing pathway and find ourselves in spiritual crisis.

With God's help and some assistance from Kierkegaard and others, I finally recognized that, for the most part, spiritual failure characterized my journey through the grieving process. This realization launched me on a quest to find a more adequate faith. While some of the emotional scarring brought about by my son's illness never would be removed, in time I received the grace to accept the inevitable and to undergo a spiritual renewal. I was led to respond to a new calling from God and embarked on a new ministry as an advocate for mentally ill persons and their families.

The five steps contained in this book are lessons learned from my journey and the experiences of many people of faith who struggled as I did and who, by God's grace, rediscovered joy after life-changing losses. The steps correspond to the main sections of the book.

*Step 1: Trust God and Rely on Others* emphasizes the decision not to attempt the journey of grief alone, but to seek comfort, strength, and guidance from God, and to allow other people to help us in our time of need.

*Step 2: Choose Reality Instead of Illusion* points out the dangers of living in denial, the hazards of pursuing various forms of escape, the risks of falling into victimism, and the possibility, with God's help, of facing the truth of our losses with courage and hope.

*Step 3: Resist the Temptation to Get Stuck* focuses on questioning, anger, and depression and warns of the perilous, seductive, and subtle desire to remain indefinitely in one or more of the stages of grief when God is nudging us to move on in order to find healing.

*Step 4: Recognize Moments of Grace* underscores the importance of identifying and appreciating the many ways God cares for us and continues to bless us even in the darkest days of our suffering.

*Step 5: Discover New Meaning and Purpose* highlights the healing we receive when we dedicate ourselves to callings born from personal tragedy, and the contentment and joy that come to us when we discover new meaning and purposes for our lives.

The most important thing for us to remember when dealing with personal grief is that we can get through it. The experience of grief, as painful as it is, is a mark of our humanity and a sign of our spiritual nature. It is a necessary journey for those who have encountered great loss and a prerequisite for those who hope to know joy and peace again. The following chapters provide practical and spiritual insight and guidance to assist people devastated by tragic losses to trust that with God's help, they too will be able to negotiate successfully their most personal journeys.

*Finding the Good in Grief: Rediscover Joy After a Life-Changing Loss* is written for all of us who have had the illusion of protection from serious harm torn away by a terrible event. It is a guide for those who need help safely negotiating the crisis of faith that so often accompanies great loss, and finding and developing the spiritual resources to survive the darkest days of grief and suffering. It is about the willingness to learn, to change, and to grow in the midst of life's difficulties, and about emotional and spiritual recovery from the devastating impact of troubles and tragedy. And it is a testimony to the mysterious power of God through faith to transform events that are experienced as radical suffering and use them for good.

Unlike a number of works dealing with faith and suffering, this book does not attempt to comfort the grieving using abstract explanations of why bad things happen to us. Rather, it explores the journey of grief in the context of faith. In the chapters that follow, after a brief discussion of a specific spiritual struggle in the midst of a particular stage of grieving, you will find a narrative that illustrates the forms of unfaith and faith that may occur along the path to recovery. The narratives dramatize ten different faces of tragedy, each corresponding to a potential stage within the grief journey.

Tragedy takes many forms, and the narratives contained in these chapters represent only a few. But those who have experienced other kinds of personal devastation are represented here nonetheless, for all tragedies have common elements. All tragedies inflict a profound sense of personal loss and suffering.

If you picked up this book, it is likely that you too have experienced a life-changing, devastating event or even a series of difficult losses in your own life. Perhaps you still are in a state of shock, or maybe you are struggling through the stages of your grief, searching to adapt and cope with the unwelcome changes tragedy has imposed on your life and the lives of those close to you.

At the end of each chapter, the "Your Story" section contains questions to help you apply the insights of the book to your own life. If your loss is recent, I recommend that you not only read this book but also answer these questions and discuss them with others. Perhaps you can find a reading partner, and the two of you can talk about the book chapter by chapter. Or as you proceed through the book, you may be able to share and discuss your thoughts and feelings with a pastor or counselor. Probably the most helpful way to study these chapters is in a grief-support group or a church-sponsored class in which readers can learn and grow spiritually as they journey together. If none of these is a practical possibility, I encourage you to write down your answers to the "Your Story" questions and to record other thoughts and feelings in a personal journal.

---

## *Your Story*

1. Read Job 3:25. What is the worst thing that ever happened to you?

2. What other unwelcomed life-changing events have you experienced? How did they change your life?

3. Look at this book's table of contents and notice the various stages of grief identified in the chapter titles. Which stage best represents where you are today?

4. What temptations have you faced during your times of grief?

5. Read Isaiah 41:10. Can you identify some ways God has cared for you during these difficulties?

# TRUST GOD AND RELY ON OTHERS

When we are experiencing personal grief, the most important thing for us to remember is that with God's help and the support of others, we can get through it.

*Weeping may remain for a night,*
*but rejoicing comes in the morning.*

PSALM 30:5

*When I am afraid,*
*I will trust in you.*

PSALM 56:3

*The widow who is really in need and left all alone puts her*
*hope in God and continues night and day to pray and*
*to ask God for help.*

1 TIMOTHY 5:5

*Encourage one another and build each other up,*
*just as in fact you are doing.*

1 THESSALONIANS 5:11

# SHOCK
## Like Being Struck by Lightning

*No man knows when his hour will come:*
*As fish are caught in a cruel net,*
*or birds are taken in a snare,*
*so men are trapped by evil times*
*that fall unexpectedly upon them.*
ECCLESIASTES 9:12

When tragedy enters our lives, it feels like we have been struck by lightning. Terrible events tend to come upon us suddenly, without warning, and they jolt us into a state of shock. This obviously is the case when the death of a loved one results from an accident, murder, or suicide. But even when we expect a loss, as in the prolonged terminal illness of someone we love, we may be caught by surprise when the end finally comes, much as we can watch a storm cloud approaching and hear the rolling thunder, yet nevertheless be traumatized when lightning strikes our house or a tree nearby.

Human beings share a primordial fear that tragic things will happen, but most of us suppress our dread. If we did not set such fears aside, we likely would be paralyzed by them and unable to carry out the simplest of tasks. So we live our daily lives believing such events are not going to occur, at least not today. Some troubled souls cannot ignore life's dangers, and raging fear cripples their daily lives. But most of the time, the rest of us are able to assume nothing bad is going to happen to us, and we are free to go about the business of living. Free, that is, until tragedy strikes in our lives.

## Emotional Numbness

Our first reaction to a life-changing loss is usually one of astonished disbelief. We tell ourselves, "This cannot be happening. There must be some mistake. There has to be another explanation." We desperately attempt to convince ourselves that "it just isn't so."

As the reality of the new information assaults our awareness, it is not uncommon for our bewildered thinking to give way to emotional numbness. We believe we should feel something, but we feel nothing. We find ourselves going through the motions of dealing with our situation, but it is as though we are standing outside ourselves, detached from all feeling, and watching ourselves as if we were observing another person. Our behavior seems robotic. It may appear to other people that our emotional flatness is inappropriate for one facing such a fearful and sad moment. But rather than being inauthentic, it is the manifestation of a human mechanism that is able to protect us during those first few dark days after a terrible, life-changing event.

Most of us have known people who appeared to be amazingly cheerful, serene, and composed after the loss of loved ones. At the time, we marveled at how well they seemed to be dealing with their grief. But after days or weeks, we may have learned these same persons were experiencing overwhelming tears and sorrow for extensive periods. Such reactions are common, and they happen for a reason.

When people lose large amounts of blood due to physical trauma, they go into a state of biological shock, and their bodily systems start to shut down. Physical shock is an indicator that a person's life is in imminent danger. The body seems to recognize that some of its organs are more important to survival than others. The shock process provides as much of the remaining blood as possible to the most important organs as a means of delaying death for as long as possible. This reaction can help an injured person survive until help arrives. Preserving the vital organs, even at the expense of other bodily systems, increases the chance of survival.

Similarly, emotional shock indicates significant danger. *A person in a state of emotional trauma may be confused and temporarily unable to safely manage his or her own life.* But as in the case of physical shock, emotional shock can also have positive value, particularly if social support systems are in place to assist those initiated into great grief. By numbing the emotional pain, the time of shock can protect and prepare a person for healing. The numbness many of us experience during the early stages of emotional shock can keep us from being overwhelmed by emotional pain, much as anesthesia prevents us from experiencing physical pain during a surgical procedure. Our brains are wondrously designed to tranquilize our emotions when we have been stunned by tragedy in order to protect us from dangerous physical and emotional reactions and buy time until we are more able to process our feelings.

**Emotional Overload**

On the other hand, numbness is not the only way some of us spontaneously react to a sudden emotional trauma. Shock also can bring with it the opposite of a robotic state, in the form of overwhelming and uncontrollable fear and anguish. These emotions can wash over us so powerfully that we cannot think rationally. Our bodies may go limp. We may become lightheaded or even faint. We may wail involuntarily for long periods of time. Like a drowning person, we may struggle against the flood of our emotions, but after a while we will likely succumb to them.

As is true for the response of numbness, *emotional outpouring can be beneficial for a brief time.* It can relieve inner stress much as a valve does when pressure builds up inside a container, and it can protectively preoccupy us in a way that prevents destructive thinking about our tragic situations.

Whether the time of shock manifests itself as numbness or as emotional overload, it is a prelude to the grieving process. It usually is of short duration, sometimes only minutes, though it also can last for several days or even weeks. Afterward, we tend to transition to what might be termed a major stage of the journey of grief, such as denial, anger, or depression. A few of us may even move directly to a state of acceptance.

Unfortunately, as the shock begins to wane, the prospect of facing and living with our emotional pain so frightens some of us that we desperately desire to prolong our initial emotional response for as long as possible. At such times, we risk subverting the healing process before it has even begun.

## Trust God and Rely on Others

The reactions and emotions that naturally come to us when we undergo great losses are gifts from God, whether or not we understand and acknowledge them as such. But the powerful emotional responses that are normal for a grieving person also come with spiritual temptations. Chief among them is the urge to go it alone—to rely on our own strength and isolate from others.

*Our success in moving toward healing depends on our willingness to trust God and rely on others.* In the early days after a life-changing loss, we need to turn to those who love us and care about us and let them provide support, guidance, and comfort. Most important of all, we need to remember that God loves us and wants us to experience healing. If with God's help we are able to face and accept our new situations, as difficult as they might be, then we can find a measure of peace within our personal storms.

## Rachel's Story

Nothing had prepared Rachel for what the doctor reported to her that day. The tumor was malignant; the cancer was spreading throughout her body. The oncologist predicted that even with treatment, Rachel could expect to live only about a year. The news threw Rachel into a state of emotional shock. She felt bewildered and disoriented.

It wasn't that Rachel was naïve. After all, she had been a nurse for more than fifteen years. She had seen many people die of cancer, had stood by the beds of numerous patients and offered comfort to families as their loved ones passed on. She understood the biology of cancer and the physical and emotional toll it takes on patients and loved ones. She had witnessed it in all types of patients from many different backgrounds. Intellectually she knew it could happen to anyone. But this was different. This was happening to her and to those she held dear.

With the news came a strange, almost out-of-body experience. For a few moments she felt detached and uninvolved. Rachel had experienced this state of being only one other time, years before, on the interstate in a freezing rain when she was riding in a car driven by a friend. The driver braked to slow down, but the car skidded off the road and down a long, steep embankment. During those few seconds of uncontrollable sliding, before the car glided between two large trees and safely stopped, Rachel thought she was about to die. Yet this thought had not been accompanied by fear. She had observed the entire event from the passenger seat as if she were in a tranquil dream.

That day in the doctor's office, she remained in a detached state as she checked out, left the office, and walked to her car. Then as she buckled her seat belt, a terrifying moment of lucidity rolled over her like a storm surge in a hurricane. A curtain within her consciousness suddenly tore apart, and Rachel found herself staring into a dark and bottomless abyss. She always had known deep within herself that the abyss was there, but she also had believed that God would take care of her and never allow her to experience such an awful thing. *There must be some mistake*, she thought. *This cannot be happening. It must be a dream.*

In her years of nursing, Rachel had come to believe that an event is tragic precisely because it is a wrenching loss of something precious. It might be the loss of security, or wholeness, or relationships, or hopes for the future. Now for Rachel it was all of the above. She was dealing with a sickness she had been told would soon end in death.

Before her tumor was discovered, Rachel had every reason to believe her life would take an expected course. She would live to see her children graduate from high school and then college. She would see them fall in love and get married. One day she would hold her grandchildren in her arms. She would have many more years of a fulfilling and compassionate vocation, caring for patients. As the years passed, she would continue to find ways to contribute to the work of her church and her community. She and her husband, David, would grow old together and travel to exotic places. Then in one moment those hopes and dreams vanished.

Rachel had the presence of mind to know she was in shock. Her training made her aware that the shock of personal tragedy is a dangerous time. She thought about calling a friend to come drive her home, but against her own better judgment, she decided she would exercise extreme caution and simply stay off the highway instead. Once on the road, however, she found it difficult to concentrate on her driving. Her mind kept rushing back to the conversation with the doctor and all of her accompanying fears. Then she spaced out, thinking about nothing and no longer feeling anything. When it registered in her consciousness that she was pulling into her own driveway, she realized she had no memory of the trip.

Her house was empty and lonely. David was at work and the children were at school. For about an hour she walked around the house in a daze. Then her fear broke through her numbness. She found herself asking God, in a loud, passionate voice, to please make it not so.

A little later, after several minutes of involuntary trembling, she decided it was not good for her to be alone. She desperately felt the need for her husband's comfort. She picked up the phone, fumbled with it, and finally dialed David's work number. She told him, between gasps for air, that she needed him to come home right away, but despite his worried questions, she refused to tell him what was going on. David recognized that Rachel had been crying and that something was terribly wrong. He told his boss there was a family emergency and hurried home.

Rachel met David as he came in the door and threw herself into his arms, sobbing uncontrollably. He held her tightly, tried to calm her, and finally obtained enough information to understand what was happening. They sat on the couch for a long time after that, while Rachel wept in his arms.

Rachel was fortunate that David was a loving, caring husband who understood the nature of the crisis he was dealing with that day. David had learned somewhere, probably in conversations with Rachel about her hospital experiences, that a person in emotional and spiritual shock needs assistance and support to get through the first few days. The wisest course for Rachel would be for her to have someone with her who could provide comfort, make mundane decisions, and assist with some of the activities of daily living. So David took a few days off from work.

Of course, David too was now in a state of shock and bewilderment. Rachel's news was the visitation of his worst nightmare. He could not yet fully comprehend what was happening to the love of his life and to his family. He needed those days off for himself as well, and he wanted to be with Rachel every second of the day.

Both of them knew this was not a time to make major decisions. That would come later. Neither was this a time to try to understand rationally the religious and spiritual significance of her condition. That too would need to wait. Yet David also had a strong feeling that they both needed some spiritual help. David called their pastor to tell him what was going on.

The following morning the pastor came to visit. After expressing his sympathy and relaying that he already had activated the church's prayer chain on Rachel's behalf, he sat silently with them for a long while.

Finally the pastor broke the silence. "I don't think anything I could say would be of much help today. I know you both are still in shock. This is not a time for us to try to make sense out of this frightening and awful news. But it *is* a time for prayer, not prayers from the mind and the mouth but simple prayers from the heart. At times like these, many people find the 'Serenity Prayer' to be one that helps the most." Then Rachel, David, and the pastor held hands and together prayed: "God, grant me the serenity to accept the things I cannot change, the courage to change the things I can, and the wisdom to know the difference."

After the prayer, the pastor said, "During the times in my life when I have been shocked by some tragic news, I have found myself praying the first line of that prayer over and over. 'God, grant me serenity. God, grant me serenity. God, grant me serenity.' Somehow I know instinctively that what I need most is to find some peace at my spiritual center. I need for the storm within me to calm enough that I can safely negotiate the time of shock and danger. I think that when misfortune suddenly strikes, it is a time to remember and cling to familiar words like those in this prayer that have been born out of the heartbreaking experiences of others."

As Rachel continued to reel in bewilderment during the early days after her diagnosis, a series of agonizing thoughts ripped through her consciousness. *What about David? How will he handle this? What about the children? What will they do? I am too young and they are far too little for this to be happening. And what about me? Am I going to lose my hair? Am I going to be in a lot of pain? How long will I really have before I am too sick to have any quality in my life?* Question after question came—only questions, no answers.

In those moments Rachel remembered to pray the Serenity Prayer. She prayed it over and over. She also found herself recalling other familiar words—words from a hymn she often sang in church:

> When through the deep waters I call thee to go,
> the rivers of sorrow shall not overflow;
> for I will be with thee, thy troubles to bless,
> and sanctify to thee thy deepest distress.[1]

The storm still swirled within her. Terror still gripped her being. But those words seemed to be something firm and stable amidst an emotional cyclone.

As the initial shock waned and the first rush of adrenalin drained, Rachel realized she had choices to make about how she would deal with her situation. Many years before, Rachel had turned to a supervisor for advice in dealing with a particularly difficult patient problem. "Let me tell you something that will save you a lot of trouble if you will heed it," her mentor had said. *"Your situation is never your problem. It is your relationship to your situation that is always your problem.* No matter what your circumstance, the first decision you will make about that situation will be to choose the attitude you are going to have toward it. Once you have done that, you will know what else to do."

In her years of hospital work, Rachel often had observed that a patient's attitude had a lot to do with the outcome of an illness. She had seen some who chose to fight their diseases for as long as possible, and she had witnessed others who surrendered to their conditions almost immediately. She had seen some patients choose to focus on their own misery; they became demanding and irritable, and caring for their needs became unpleasant for everyone. She also had taken care of some seriously ill patients who remained cheerful, appreciative, and sensitive to others. They seemed unwilling to complain, even when their conditions appeared unbearable.

Rachel also had been involved in several cases of inexplicable, even miraculous, recoveries. She believed she had seen firsthand the power of prayer and of a positive spiritual attitude in the healing process. She understood and took seriously what the physician had told her, yet she also believed that only God knew whether there was a chance she could beat her cancer. And she believed that remission was possible, even at this late stage in her condition. She knew that her church's prayer chain already had been activated and that colleagues at work were praying for her.

Rachel decided to face the reality of her condition while steadfastly holding on to her hope. She thought about her husband and children, about the patients at the hospital who still needed her services. And Rachel decided that she was not going to be one of those people who just gives up. She knew the treatment for her disease would be incredibly uncomfortable. Her hair would fall out. She would experience constant nausea and weakness. But she determined to do whatever it took to fight her disease.

The best-case scenario, of course, would be a cure, perhaps occurring mysteriously as what the medical community knows as a spontaneous remission. Or perhaps it would come from a new medical breakthrough while she was buying a few more months with her radiation and chemotherapy treatments. Rachel decided she would hang on to those hopes as long as she could. But if in the end she was still going to die, then she was committed to squeezing as much quality out of life as possible and to being the best mother, wife, and nurse manager she could be under the circumstances.

Rachel also decided that each day she would try to focus on the positives. She would attempt to stay grateful and pleasant in her attitude. She knew that if she did not survive, it would be unbelievably hard on those who loved her and depended on her. She wanted their burdens to be as light as possible. Rachel decided to symbolize her intentional relationship to her personal tragedy by shopping for and purchasing an attractive wig. Then she went to the beauty shop, had all her hair shaved off, and began wearing the wig.

Having prayerfully decided how she intended to deal with her condition, Rachel asked God to help her remain faithful to the path she had chosen. As the weeks and months went by, some days were more difficult than others. But her family and friends all marveled at her determination and spirit. This was so even as she suffered through all her treatments, including a highly experimental one that made her especially sick.

Despite the side effects, the treatments slowed the disease and helped make it possible for Rachel to spend some irreplaceable times with her family. She and David took the children on a trip to the Grand Canyon. They attended a large family reunion. They spent almost every other weekend at their mountain cabin together. In the midst of all of this, Rachel continued to work most days. She took extended sick leave only after fifteen months of battling with her illness. But despite her amazing faith and courage in the face of her devastating disease, Rachel eventually declined rapidly, and eighteen months after she received the diagnosis from her doctor, Rachel died.

Rachel's memorial service was standing room only. She was remembered as a woman of faith who faced her personal tragedy with great courage and grace. As her pastor concluded his message, he reminded those present that the sudden onset of Rachel's disease came as a shock to everyone who knew her as the youthful, vibrant person she was.

"None of us knows what tomorrow might bring," he said. "Such things can happen to any of us at any time and when we least expect them. We can only hope that if and when they do, we will be as persistent in our hope as Rachel was. Until very close to the end, she held on to her hope for healing in this life. When it was clear that her time was drawing near, she held on just as fervently to her hope of heaven.

"Eighteen months ago, just after Rachel and David received the news of her diagnosis, I prayed with them in their family room. We stood together, held hands, and recited the Serenity Prayer. Rachel not only prayed that prayer, she lived it. Throughout her ordeal, she remained a person of faith. She turned to God every day and prayed for the serenity to calm her anxiety, for comfort in the midst of her suffering, for courage in the face of her illness, and for guidance in deciding how to make the best use of each moment. She rejected self-pity and resentment as unacceptable options. She demonstrated a gentle and caring spirit in her relationships with those around her. Through it all, she did everything she could to fight her disease, but she trusted God with the outcome.

"We have much to learn from Rachel. Her life instructs us on how to face disease and death with courage and how to trust God and rely on others even in the most difficult of circumstances."

## Your Story

1. Read Ecclesiastes 9:12. Recall when you first found out about a life-changing loss. How would you describe your feelings at the time?

2. What makes a state of shock dangerous? What can you do to reduce the danger?

3. What descriptive words would you use to characterize the attitude Rachel had toward her diagnosed disease? What are some other attitudes people have when facing similar circumstances?

4. What familiar words did Rachel find sustaining in her time of trouble? Read Psalm 56:3. What other verses of Scripture or lines from hymns do you recall that might be helpful during a similar time?

5. Whom among your friends, family, and social networks would you be willing to rely on for emotional support and guidance during a time of personal crisis?

# CHOOSE REALITY INSTEAD OF ILLUSION

If we allow ourselves to live in the illusions of denial, escape, or fantasy, we stray from the pathway to healing. With God's help we can face reality, live in the truth, and adapt to our losses, even in the midst of their devastation.

*My soul is weary with sorrow;*
*strengthen me according to your word.*
*Keep me from deceitful ways.*
PSALM 119:28–29


*Do you want to get well?*
JOHN 5:6


*Do not fear, for I am with you;*
*do not be dismayed, for I am your God.*
*I will strengthen you and help you;*
*I will uphold you with my righteous right hand.*
ISAIAH 41:10


*I have no greater joy than to hear that my children*
*are walking in the truth.*
3 JOHN 1:4

## 3

# DENIAL
### It's Not a River in Egypt

*When an overwhelming scourge sweeps by,*
*it cannot touch us,*
*for we have made a lie our refuge*
*and falsehood our hiding place.*
ISAIAH 28:15

Soon after we are struck by the initial shock of a life-changing loss, it is common to enter a more or less extended period of denial. When we are still in shock, disbelief can be a normal, involuntary response. As this reaction begins to wane and reality intrudes upon our consciousness, *we may attempt to maintain our disbelief for as long as possible.*

At some level of our being, we know the truth, but we are unwilling to face it. We assume that by refusing to acknowledge it, we are protected from its implications. We attempt to convince ourselves that we can continue to experience life much as it was before the tragic event occurred. We do this because denial softens the blow and postpones for a time the overwhelming pain and devastating change in a person's life that come with a loss. As such, denial can be a temporary blessing.

### The Two Levels

Many of us go through two levels of denial: primary and secondary. Initially, we enter *primary denial,* in which we refuse to recognize that a tragic event has occurred or is about to occur and that a problem requiring action exists. We cling to the illusion that it could not be happening to *us*.

The prophets of the Old Testament spoke out many times against the illusions of false security on the part of the kings and leaders of Israel and Judah.[2] When the northern kingdom of Israel was facing impending doom, Amos chided the men of nobility because they trampled the poor yet felt secure in the holy places. Isaiah reproached the kings and their advisors in the southern kingdom of Judah for "making a lie their refuge," because they were unwilling to recognize the faithlessness of Judah and the threat of Assyrian might. Again and again, the covenanted people misinterpreted their chosen status as insulation against suffering. They refused to believe terrible things could happen to them.

I am fairly certain I would have recognized the truth of my son's condition when he first showed signs of his mental illness if I had witnessed his symptoms in someone else's child. But I did not believe such a terrible thing could ever afflict one of my own children. I remember trying to explain the symptoms away as adolescent behavior, even though I should have known better. At an unconscious level I was refusing to see what was clearly before me.

Primary denial is usually followed by *secondary denial*. Secondary denial occurs when the realities of our situation make it impossible to maintain primary denial. A person in secondary denial admits that a problem exists but minimizes the serious nature of it. In place of the delusions of invincibility that accompany primary denial, secondary denial constructs counterfeit hopes. Our main desire at this point is to find a way to reverse what has happened. This often takes the form of bargaining, when we make radical promises to God if he will only make things the way they used to be.

When I could no longer maintain an outright denial of my son's illness, I convinced myself it was a temporary condition that could be reversed. I began to look for a quick and promising cure. I found a private psychiatric hospital that was more than willing to promise me a miracle in exchange for a very large sum of money. Wanting desperately to believe their assurances, I borrowed everything I could, even taking out a second mortgage on our home, and drove my son to the facility, where they kept him for six weeks. When he came home, he was a little better, but in a matter of days he deteriorated to his prehospital state. Nothing was different, except that I was now impoverished, a condition that eventually led to our losing the house.

## Living in Illusion

We will often go to great lengths to defend and reinforce our states of denial. We all know an ostrich does not make danger go away by burying its head in the sand. Yet we human beings are similarly inclined to construct delusional defenses around our lucidity when threatened by dangers or touched by human tragedies.

Whenever events in life put cracks in our illusions, we work as hard as we can to patch them up. We use just about anything—the psychological and spiritual equivalents of Band-Aids, bailing wire, and masking tape—until real life makes such frantic efforts no longer possible.

After someone dear to us dies, for example, we may expect the deceased to walk through the door at any time, as if he or she has been away on a journey. Sometimes we set an extra place at the table; we may refuse to touch closets containing a loved one's clothes. Bedrooms, particularly children's rooms, may remain for many years as they were at the time of death. We may look for our loved one in a crowd of strangers and hope to hear his or her voice each time the phone rings.

While these images evoke empathy, there is a fundamental problem with living in denial. Emotional healing and constructive action are virtually impossible as long as the reality of a serious problem goes unrecognized and unacknowledged. Denial is seductive because for a while it feels so much better than going through what we suspect will be unbearable pain. Denial is insidious because self-deceit is so difficult to recognize. How easily we recognize the denial of others, and how difficult it is to see our own!

## Delayed Healing

While denial can offer a degree of temporary comfort, it carries great risks. This can be seen clearly if we think of a person who has a very serious physical symptom and refuses to see a physician. The illusion that the disease is not real unless it has been diagnosed is clung to for as long as possible. Often such people end up facing serious disability or premature death which could have been avoided if they had sought help when symptoms first appeared.

Denial can also delay the interventions necessary to deal with addictions or marital problems. The unwillingness to acknowledge the existence of a problem has long been a key strategy of addicted persons for avoiding change. They continually work to convince themselves that they are not hooked on their drugs and can continue to abuse their substances without serious consequences. The first step toward any possible recovery for such people is to admit that they are addicts.

Similarly, the signs of an unfaithful spouse can be ignored for years, preventing the intervention needed for a healthy solution to an unhealthy relationship. As long as the problem can be ignored successfully, the discomfort associated with intervention can be avoided. *Living in denial is easier in the short run than facing a problem and taking the often difficult and painful actions necessary to address it. But in the long run, denial can be a recipe for disaster.* This is equally true for a person who has experienced the loss of a loved one. The longer we are in denial about the reality and implications of a death, the unhealthier denial can become for us. Death brings about the necessity for change in the lives of those of us left behind, creating a void in our lives. The person we have lost was unique and irreplaceable. The relationship we had, the time we spent together, and our mutual participation in activities and events cannot be duplicated.

Such losses require constructive alternatives for how we spend our time and with whom. Sometimes we face an urgent need for change in our living situation due to economic or safety concerns. In any case, prolonged denial prevents us from facing not only the loss we have experienced but the life decisions necessitated by that loss as well. As long as we maintain a state of denial, it is unlikely that we will adapt successfully to our new situation.

## A God of Truth

Denial is a God-given coping mechanism that cushions the shock of a great personal loss. But denial can become a form of unfaith when it is chosen as a long-term strategy. Such unwillingness to face reality may indicate a lack of trust in God's ability as our Shepherd to see us through the dark valleys of our troubles.[3] Consequently, our denial can delay and sometimes prevent altogether the healing God desires to bestow on us.

God is a God of truth. He calls us to be truthful in our social interactions and truthful with ourselves. God is capable of helping us face the truth, no matter how horrible it may appear. And he is capable of helping us adapt to the truth, no matter how challenging the life changes that might be required.

Because God wants us to face reality rather than hide from it, he seeks to break through our denial so that we might find healing. We may not feel like we are being cared for, but whether events or people penetrate and shatter the shell of our denial, it is God who is lovingly at work, and it is God who is offering to help us recover from our grief and continue the journey we are intended to take.

## Tanya's Story

Tanya noticed that Keisha was a good bit slower than her other children had been, but she assumed her youngest daughter eventually would catch up. *Some children mature faster than others,* she thought. *It isn't anything to worry about.* But when Keisha started preschool, her teachers suspected a problem right away and requested Tanya's written permission to have Keisha tested.

Tanya assumed the papers were routine and signed them without concern, but a few weeks later, the results sent Tanya into a state of shock. Suddenly, all her hopes for Keisha were dashed. One day other children in the preschool would go off to college and then begin to live independent lives. But Keisha would always be an emotional child with moderate mental retardation. Stunned, Tanya suddenly had a vision of the future where she and her husband were sentenced to a lifetime of parenting and caregiving, and the caregiving would become more difficult with time and age until it became physically impossible. *Then what will happen?* she wondered. She knew that many individuals with moderate mental retardation live their adult lives in group homes that provide supportive care. But at the moment, Tanya could not bear the thought of Keisha living out her life that way, and a profound sense of sadness engulfed her. She felt cheated out of a daughter and out of her own life.

It was all too painful to contemplate. So Tanya stopped thinking about it. She refused to accept the results of the developmental evaluation. It was not a rational decision on Tanya's part, but it was a decision nonetheless. She went back to her daily routine. With grim determination, she changed nothing. She spent her days just as she had before. Not once did she allow herself to believe anything had changed. Whenever she was asked about her daughter, she became irritated but managed to change the subject politely. After that first period of shock, she did not shed a single tear. After all, as long as everything remained as it had been, there was nothing to cry about.

Many weeks went by. Then one day the preschool director called and asked Tanya to show up for an emergency conference before school the next morning. At the meeting, Tanya was told that Keisha could no longer remain in a mainstream preschool. Keisha could not keep up with the work. She had little or no impulse control and had bitten two of her classmates, and previously, the teacher and the teacher's aide. Something had to be done.

Tanya attempted to reason with the teachers. "She is only three," she said. "Lots of children go through a biting stage. I will talk to her about the biting." But the staff felt strongly that Keisha needed specialized services in a self-contained classroom with a special education teacher.

For the first time since hearing the results of Keisha's initial evaluation,

Tanya felt a crack in her emotional armor. No longer could she successfully withhold all her tears. From that point forward, she found it impossible to maintain what had been a virtually impenetrable denial of the reality of Keisha's condition. After an agonizing night, she informed the director of the preschool that she would agree to the self-contained class.

Tanya was not comfortable with her decision. In her heart, she still hoped the experts were wrong and that Keisha, with a little help, could grow out of this developmental thing. She was willing for the moment to recognize that there was a problem, but she was not ready to believe it was going to be serious and long-term.

Soon Tanya began to make the rounds of various pediatricians, psychologists, and child-development centers, determined to find some authority who would declare the original evaluation wrong. Everyone agreed with the results of the original evaluation.

Next Tanya began to search the Internet for possible miracle cures. She looked into vitamin therapy and growth hormones. She even fed her daughter some natural supplements for a while, until she heard a warning on television about the effects of unregulated supplements on young children.

Week after week, she asked her church to pray for a miracle, that God would heal Keisha's brain and cause it to develop normally. She took Keisha to a church a hundred miles away, where a preacher laid hands on the child and prayed. For more than a week afterward, Tanya believed that Keisha had been cured. But the reality soon sank in. Nothing had changed.

Tanya became even more frantic to find something to change the situation. She prayed and prayed. In her prayers she tried to strike a deal with God. If God would make Keisha OK, then Tanya would give up desserts and shopping or whatever else God wanted her to give up. She would give them up forever. She even offered to take upon herself some terrible disease or disability, if only her child would be made whole. She promised to go to church every Sunday and to do whatever God wanted her to do. "Please tell me, God, what I have to do," she prayed, "and I will do it."

The answer to Tanya's prayer did not come in the form of a cure. It came one night in the words of her husband, who had grown weary of the time, energy, and money Tanya spent chasing a cure. "You want to know what God wants you to do?" he asked. "I'll tell you what God wants you to do. God wants you to accept the fact that Keisha is retarded and will always be retarded. I'm sure God heals lots of people. Even the doctors talk about miraculous cures they can't explain. But if a little girl has an arm cut off and it is not possible to sew it back on, she won't grow another one, no matter how much everyone prays for her. And if Keisha was born with a brain that doesn't work right, then I think it is going to stay that way. We need to get focused on how we all can live with her disability and on getting Keisha the training she needs to have as good a life as possible. We need to stop chasing what is never going to happen." He then turned over and went to sleep.

The words cut deeply. At some profoundly hidden place in her being, Tanya knew he was right, and she cried for most of a sleepless night. She had no idea that all those tears were bottled up inside her. By morning she felt hurt, exhausted, and washed out but also strangely relieved.

Months later, with the help of friends in a support group for parents of children with mental retardation, Tanya would look back on her months in denial and gain insight into her journey.

"While denial is a natural coping mechanism," Tanya's group leader had said, "a person who has cut an artery and is in denial could quickly bleed to death. Denial often delays critical early interventions and necessary actions to address very real problems."

The support group helped Tanya focus on learning more about mental retardation and the services that could help her daughter. As a consequence, she became better able to devote her energies to the difficult task of parenting and to securing the appropriate professional resources and educational programming her daughter needed.

One Sunday, almost a year after her husband had penetrated her defenses with what felt like harsh words at the time, their pastor preached a sermon called "Denial: It's Not a River in Egypt." He told about King David and other people in the Bible who tried to live in denial and who needed prophets to get them to face reality.[4]

"Denial," the pastor continued, "even if it is expressed as religious hope, is a type of unfaith. It is a refusal to face reality, the reality of God's universe where pain and suffering are a part of life. It is an unwillingness to acknowledge and respond in faith to our unique, tragic experiences, as God in compassion intends for us to do. It is a spiritual blindness. It shields us from the emotional pain of viewing tragic reality. But it also blocks us from the spiritual resources available to us as people of faith during such times.

"Denial is an escape from the life that God has called a person of faith to live. It is a hiding not only from a particularly unpleasant reality but also from the fullness of creation in which God has placed us. The created universe is filled with a multitude of unpleasant realities. And living in denial is a failure of the spirit to hear and receive God's Word that in all things God's grace is sufficient."

It was an important moment of clarity for Tanya. Just as the people in biblical days needed prophets to break through their denial, she had needed others to break through her illusions.

The pastor had pointed out that when people's lives are addressed by prophets in times of denial, the experience can be traumatic. Tanya remembered the first time she learned of Keisha's retardation and how angry it had made her. And the night her husband penetrated her secondary denial, Tanya was more angry and hurt with him than she had ever been. She stayed angry with him for days. But she could not go back to the way it was before.

The pastor also said something that gave Tanya a whole new perspective on her experience: "It is the grace of God that allows us to face our sufferings realistically, to accept them and deal with them constructively." For Tanya, the agents of that grace were those who dared to penetrate her denial. In doing so, they became God's instruments as they opened up new possibilities for the future, both for her and her daughter.

As he concluded, the pastor also had a word that morning for those who had not yet faced a serious tragedy in their lives: "Spiritual preparation before tragedy strikes sometimes can mean that external intervention is unnecessary. A person of faith can pray for the insight and honesty to recognize the temptation to live in denial when tragedy comes and the courage to resist its seduction. And a person of faith also can pray for the assurance that denial is unnecessary, because absolutely nothing is so terrible that it cannot be faced with God's comfort, support, and guidance. Let us remember the words of the apostle Paul in 2 Corinthians 1:3–4: 'Praise be to the God and Father of our Lord Jesus Christ, the Father of compassion and the God of all comfort, who comforts us in all our troubles, so that we can comfort those in any trouble with the comfort we ourselves have received from God.'

"And what if our spiritual preparation is inadequate for the magnitude of the tragedy? What if, despite our efforts to avoid it, we slip into denial? Faith requires us to recognize that when the smashing of our illusions comes, through whatever agents, it is the compassionate activity of God. God is calling us back to reality and to his comforting care. And that care will surely come, for God will not forsake us in our time of need. The only question is, what will we do when that time comes?"

"What indeed!" Tanya said quietly. She was grateful for her husband's words and glad she had found a support group of people who had been through their own times of denial. She knew that she had probably gotten through her denial much more quickly than she would have without those people. And she was amazed at the relief she felt at not having to shore up her self-deceptions any longer.

### Your Story

1.  Can you recall a time when you or someone you know was in denial about a problem? What were you or they refusing to accept?

2. Tanya's husband and others challenged her denial. Can you think of an example when God used someone to call you or another person out of denial?

3. What is the difference between primary and secondary denial? Can you remember a time when you were tempted to bargain with God or to put your trust in unrealistic hopes?

4. Why do you think God wants you to choose reality over illusion? Read 3 John 1:4. How does this verse help you answer the question?

5. Read Psalm 119:29 and Isaiah 41:10. How do the writer of the psalm and the prophet Isaiah deal with the problem of denial? What does this mean to you?

4

# ESCAPE
## You Can Run but You Will Only Get Tired

*Where can I go from your Spirit?*
*Where can I flee from your presence?*
*If I go up to the heavens, you are there;*
*If I make my bed in the depths, you are there.*
PSALM 139:7–8

When most of God's creatures experience danger, they choose either *fight* or *flight* as a survival strategy. Human beings are no exception. When faced with a threat, we generally choose to either struggle with the challenge or attempt to escape. Who among us, when we have perceived a perilous situation, has not experienced an aggressive impulse or else the urge to run away?

In the early days of my son's mental illness, when I was scared, bewildered, and overwhelmed, I sometimes found myself fantasizing about running off to some safe and peaceful place. I wanted to escape my emotional pain, to go where I would no longer have to think about what was happening to him or deal with his frightening behavior.

In the face of emotional suffering, there is nothing wrong with feeling the desire to escape. Such feelings are a natural response. Depending on the conditions, neither is there anything intrinsically wrong with actually taking a break from the intensity of one's grief. Such respite can be helpful to the healing process.

Society tends to associate *fight* with courage and *flight* with coward-ice. But in reality *fight* can be a foolish response, and *flight*, a wise one. The best generals know how to advance their armies when conditions are favorable and how to retreat, if necessary, in order to fight another day.

## Temporary Retreats

*A temporary escape can be beneficial* because it offers respite from emo-tional exhaustion and postpones dealing with the overwhelming prac-tical problems that come with a great loss. Sometimes the wisest thing a grieving person can do is go to another place for a while, geographically or mentally.

Of course, *whether fight or flight is the right strategy depends on time and circumstance.* This point is well illustrated in biblical narratives. When Moses killed the Egyptian slave master, he fled to the land of Midian. After a long time, God spoke to Moses from a burning bush, and Moses returned to Egypt, where he repeatedly challenged Pharaoh to let the Hebrew people go. Elijah the prophet confronted and defeated the priests of Baal in a life-or-death contest on Mount Carmel. But when Jezebel threatened to murder him, Elijah fled into the desert to a cave on Mount Horeb. Then, when God spoke to the prophet in a "gentle whis-per," Elijah was sent back to face his enemies once again.[5]

In both stories, it is clear that it was God who led these prophets to their places of retreat and God who cared for them there. And it was God who, in God's time, called these prophets to return and face their enemies.

From a faith perspective, there are times when God knows we need to flee from the trials and tribulations of the world to our own versions of a desert retreat. Such a place could be the home of relatives or friends, where we feel safe and where others can help care for our needs. Perhaps we have a special vacation place, such as in the mountains, beside a lake, or at a beach, where past experiences tell us that if we spend some time there, we can expect to regain our spiritual serenity. Or maybe there is a place in our imagination, possibly a scene we remember from our childhood or a setting we have wished for in our hearts. When we close our eyes, each of us has the capacity to visit our own special places to find calm for our stormy souls.

But whether our retreats are geographical or mental, the time inevitably comes when it is no longer a good thing for us to remain in our places of refuge. There is no such thing as a long-term geographical cure for grief, because we take our heartaches with us wherever we go. And mental journeys cannot be sustained for long, because the realities of our everyday lives and the hurts within us intrude and demand attention.

*Retreats are intended to be temporary respites.* They can assist us in preparing for the difficulties we must face. In times of tragedy, they can help begin the healing process, but they cannot complete it. For that to happen, we must face our losses and allow God to lead us through the dark valleys of our grief.

That is why God calls us to return and confront head-on the reasons for our withdrawal. If we listen, God speaks to us when our season of respite is over and assures us that he is with us to help us in our struggles.

It is, of course, common to want to stay in a place of refuge indefinitely. Just as the disciple Peter wanted to remain on the mountaintop of the transfiguration but had to come down and face his time of trial,[6] so we also desire to remain in retreat for as long as possible but are called instead to return to the real world to face our difficulties.

### Dangerous Paths

While temporary retreats can be therapeutic, *not all escape routes lead to healing.* Some of the paths we choose in order to flee from emotional pain lead to increased suffering. This is especially true when our difficulties have been caused by our own selfish and irresponsible behaviors.

The narrative about Adam and Eve hiding from God in the garden after eating the fruit of the forbidden tree[7] is the story of every child who has ever disobeyed a parent and tried to avoid the consequences. Most of us agree that when children are not held accountable, they seldom grow up to be responsible members of society. And when adults attempt to escape responsibility for their harmful actions, they often compound the suffering of others while continuing down a slippery slope of their own making.

But what about the desire to run away when faced with tragic circumstances *not* of our own making? While a temporary retreat can be beneficial, if we try to flee when we are supposed to stay and face our time of trial, or if we choose a potentially self-destructive method of escape, we soon discover that our troubles follow us and multiply. There are many such dangerous paths.

One of the more common forms of escape is the use of tranquilizers, painkillers, and alcohol. It is a means of dealing with grief that can come with a great cost. When we are distraught, we are at increased risk of abuse and addiction.

Overeating is another typical strategy. The initial shock of a personal loss frequently destroys the desire to eat. But when our shock begins to ease, many of us turn to comfort foods in order to reduce our sense of pain. Consequently, it is not unusual for some of us to gain a considerable amount of weight following a personal loss.

We would be remiss if we did not also mention the potential to escape into sexual activity. The loneliness and insecurity we experience during a time of grief can be overwhelming. If we have lost a spouse to divorce or death, we soon may find ourselves, as the country song suggests, "looking for love in all the wrong places."

Other forms of sensual escape can be as seemingly benign as going on a shopping binge, watching a great deal of television, playing video games for hours on end, or indulging in excessive sleep. Despite rationalizations to the contrary, any type of sensuality carries great risks for grieving persons and can delay the healing process indefinitely.

*In times of loss and emotional pain, it is important to seek God's guidance.* Temptation is most powerful when we are most vulnerable. If we are seduced by an unhealthy form of escape, it can lead to disaster. If we retreat in order to prepare for what is to come but overstay the time of

our return, we can seriously delay and even prevent the long-term healing we need. In either case, we are choosing to live in unfaith. But if we
trust that God's love is with us in our time of grief and that God's Spirit
will provide comfort and guidance sufficient to our needs, then we can
freely make the decisions and take the actions necessary to negotiate
our journey successfully.

## Wayne's Story

Wayne, a successful graphic artist, had recently purchased a beautiful
new home in a peaceful neighborhood where he and his wife hoped to
raise a family. Then one Monday morning, Wayne was told that his company was downsizing and he was no longer employed.

At first, Wayne felt confident he would find another job quickly. But
after a few weeks of making calls and submitting applications, he became discouraged. Soon his wife, Jeanie, who had not worked outside
their home for several years, went back to work as a temporary office
assistant at minimum wage. Despite her contribution to the family fi-
nances, the bills were piling up.

Wayne began to feel hopeless, with no sense of security or hope for
the future. Such dark and negative feelings were extremely uncomfortable. Wayne hated the way he felt, and he wanted to feel good again.

Earlier in his life, Wayne had dealt with unpleasant emotions by turning to alcohol. But with the help of AA, Wayne had gotten sober. Only
a few months after joining AA, he met Jeanie, and with her encouragement he dedicated his life to Christ and joined a church. A year later, he
dropped out of AA. Because he was active in church and trying to live
a Christian life, he considered his drinking days to be far behind him.
Now the thought of having a beer occurred to him, but he managed to
put it out of his mind. Soon, however, Wayne found another way to deal
with his personal pain.

For a long time, he had wanted a large truck with off-road capability,
and one day he decided that having one might alleviate his unhappiness.
While Jeanie was at work, and without discussing it with her, he traded

his old car for the truck of his dreams. The payments were more than twice those for the car. A few weeks later, he backed a top-of-the-line bass boat—also bought on credit—into the garage. But because Wayne's credit was now marginal, the interest rates on his new purchases were exorbitant. He was upside-down on the truck and boat before he had made a single payment.

Furthermore, new card offers came in the mail each day, and after being laid off, Wayne had applied for some of them. It felt like free money to him. The mail also was filled with bills. Wayne threw them unopened into a desk drawer. Sometimes when he needed spending money, he wrote a check. Soon the checks began to bounce.

When Jeanie realized what was happening, she was filled with panic. The couple argued. Wayne stormed out and went fishing. Jeanie desperately tried to repair the damage as best she could. But there was not enough money. Bill collectors called continuously. Wayne made promises he knew he could not keep just to end the annoyance temporarily. Within a few months, both the new boat and the truck had been repossessed.

Wayne's fishing days had ended, and he began to sleep late. When he got up, he did not bother to shave. For most of the day, he sat in his family room with the shades drawn, watching television. Jeanie came home each day to a kitchen filled with dirty dishes and a cluttered house. She had been tolerant at first, but she soon began to feel resentment, and one day she and Wayne argued heatedly. Wayne drove off in Jeanie's car and did not return until four in the morning. Jeanie could smell the alcohol before he reached the bed.

From that day forward, Jeanie always came home to find Wayne surrounded by beer cans. And as soon as Jeanie arrived each day, Wayne left and did not return until the early morning. Some nights, Jeanie thought she smelled perfume along with the smell of alcohol. The two of them could not talk any more without arguing. Jeanie now was terrified. Wayne was too, and it took more and more booze to bury his feelings of impending doom.

In desperation, Jeanie woke Wayne late one Sunday morning and told him she was planning to leave him. That got Wayne's attention. They spent the day talking about all their difficulties. In the end, Jeanie agreed to give Wayne a chance to save their marriage. And Wayne agreed to take some serious action. The first thing he did was call his old AA sponsor, Hal. They met at a local diner for a cup of coffee that same evening.

"You look terrible," Hal said. "What's going on?"

Wayne described his job loss, his spending, the repossessions, the tension with Jeanie, the boozing, and the one-night stands. "It's such a mess. I've dug a deep hole for myself, and I don't think there is any way to climb out."

"First things first," Hal said. "Do you want to get well?"

Wayne was not surprised by the question, though it made him intensely uncomfortable. Hal had asked him the same question a long time ago when they first met at a Friday night meeting. Wayne also recognized it as a question Jesus once asked a paralyzed man, according to the gospel of John.[8] Wayne sensed where Hal was going with it. "Of course I do. I wouldn't be here if I didn't. But I don't know where to start."

"If you want to get well," Hal said, "you can't lie around waiting for someone to rescue you from your own folly. You wouldn't be in this condition if you simply had taken the action that was necessary when you first lost your job instead of running away and hiding from your troubles. Think about it. How has running from your troubles worked for you?"

"Terrible."

"That's right," Hal responded. "If you had done then what you needed to do, you wouldn't have nearly the troubles you have now. But there is nothing to be gained by wringing your hands over *should have* and *might have* or by punishing yourself with self-blame. If you want things to be better, the first thing you have to do is to get out of the booze."

Wayne wondered if it was any longer possible for him to quit drinking. His alcoholism had become much worse this second time around. But he knew Hal was right. His life had no chance of getting better as long as he remained under the power of his addiction.

"And if you're going to get out of the booze," Hal continued, "you're going to have to go with me to a meeting tonight, pick up a white chip, and make ninety meetings in ninety days. That's the only way I'm going to work with you again. There are a lot of things you can do after you get out of the booze, but the first thing you have to do is stop running from your troubles. And right now that means you get sober. You aren't even able to think clearly right now because your addiction is thinking for you."

Wayne stayed sober during those first three months, but his resolve to live an alcohol-free life was still shaky. That is why Hal took Wayne to a regional AA conference.

One of the speakers at the conference identified himself as a person of faith who nevertheless had become an alcoholic. "Persons of faith," he said, "do not have immunity from the desire to run from reality. And there are many ways to run. My way was the bottle. It is important to understand that any form of running from reality is a running away from God. The problem with running from our troubles is that when we do, we just make matters worse. We soon learn that *we can run, but we will only get tired.*"

As Wayne listened, he had to admit he felt tired. In fact, he was exhausted. He knew it was time to quit running away, to face his difficulties and do something constructive about them. But his confidence was gone. Was he up to the challenge?

Then the speaker said something that Wayne would recall as a defining moment in his life: "It is ironic that we tend to run from God when we need God the most. It is an even greater irony that God loves us and desires that we turn to our loving Creator in times of trouble. The good news is that there is no place to go that God has not gone before us. *There is no place we can run to that is so far away that God is not already there and waiting to give us aid, if only we become willing to ask for help.* Whenever we feel tempted to run from the pain of our difficulties, it is a sign that we need to pray for strength, for serenity, and for guidance."

Wayne purchased a recording of the presentation, and he listened to it again and again. As he meditated on the talk, Wayne was able to admit to himself that he could not stay sober and face his problems alone. The good news was—he did not have to.

Once he had some sobriety under his belt and was experiencing some spiritual centeredness, Wayne was able to take some other actions to begin to address his problems. With Hal's help, Wayne decided it was time to come to terms with the fact that he was not going to get another graphic-artist job in the area. It was time to look for some other kind of work. After putting in many applications, he was hired as a management trainee at a fast-food restaurant. It was not the kind of work he would have chosen, and it did not pay nearly as well as his old job. But it was work, and he could finally provide some much-needed additional income. He and Jeanie visited a financial counselor. With her help, the couple was able to develop a budget and a plan for dealing with their debts.

Almost a year after that initial meeting with Hal, Wayne himself was asked to speak at an AA meeting. He told the group that he had learned something new and life-changing through his troubles. "When I lost my job, I thought God had abandoned me," he said. "I was wrong. It was I who abandoned God. Like the prodigal son in the Bible, I was the one who ran away from my heavenly Father, my Higher Power, to squander all the blessings I had received.[9] God had given me a new reality, the reality of a lost job. I abandoned God when I refused to face the reality that God had given me. I ran away from God because I didn't want to face that reality. I wanted a different reality. So I turned again to alcohol and to every other temporary pleasure I could find.

"But God didn't give up on me. God had given me a wonderful wife who would not put up with my foolishness. He gave me a great sponsor who does not let me get away with anything other than rigorous honesty with myself and with others. My Higher Power has given me the beginnings of a new recovery and a new experience of his spiritual presence in my life. I still have terrible credit. I continue to have financial difficulties. But with God's help, I am facing my difficulties. One day at a time, things are getting better.

"I have found it is never too late to trust that God will hear our prayers and come to our aid," Wayne said. "One day at a time, I am trying to live in reality and to live in trust, for I believe God keeps promises and that 'God is our refuge and strength, an ever-present help in trouble' (Ps. 46:1).

"In conclusion, let me leave you with this question: Is there some reality that you are unwilling to face today?"

---

## *Your Story*

1. Where is a good, safe place for you to retreat temporarily from your troubles?

2. What unhealthy escape routes tempt you when you are afraid or in emotional pain?

3. How does running from problems make them worse? Give examples of where you have seen or experienced this truth.

4. Read Psalm 46:1. Can you give examples of God helping you and others leave behind destructive behaviors and return to responsible living?

5. How close do you feel you are to God right now? Read Psalm 139:7–8. According to this Scripture, how close is God to you?

# 5

# VICTIMISM
## Where's a Superhero When You Really Need One?

*Three times I pleaded with the Lord to take it away from me.*
*But he said to me, "My grace is sufficient for you, for my power*
*is made perfect in weakness."*
2 CORINTHIANS 12:8–9

When we learn from the evening news about a terrible event such as a deadly tornado that has plowed through a residential community, we often describe the dead, the wounded, and those who have lost loved ones and valuable property as *victims*. Such a term seems appropriate because the individuals touched by those events did not have the ability to prevent them from happening.

*When we are not responsible for our own suffering, understanding ourselves as victims may be beneficial.* It is unrealistic and unhealthy to assume we have the power to protect ourselves and those we love from *all* harm. And it is self-defeating to assume blame for circumstances beyond our control. When we do, we compound the already overwhelming burdens of our losses.

*While it may be helpful at times to think of ourselves as victims, it also can be detrimental.* The preceding chapters have shown how getting stuck in a particular grief reaction can postpone and even prevent healing. Victimism—a contemporary term for living life from the mindset of a victim—is no exception. If we are struggling with feelings of powerlessness and guilt, a long-term victim role may be especially seductive.

**Powerlessness**

When we become victims of some terrible event beyond our control, we usually have an overwhelming sense of powerlessness. Most of us like to think we are in control of the circumstances of our lives and that if we are smart enough and do all the right things, nothing bad can happen. We may know better in our hearts. We may witness the innocent suffering of others. Yet we remain confident that such things will not happen to us. Then when they do, the illusion of our ability to control our lives, particularly our security, is shattered.

Powerlessness is not a pleasant sensation. We feel defeated and sapped of our strength. We question our own abilities and find it difficult to trust others. For example, a woman who has endured a violent crime such as rape may live with the terror that comes from feeling vulnerable and defenseless despite any safety measures she takes. She may add locks to her doors and windows, install a security system, and stay awake at night. But every protective action she employs serves to underscore her sense of being robbed of power over her own body and her own life.

But just as it is a fantasy to believe we can secure our lives against all potential harm, it also is an illusion to believe that any outside force or event can rob us permanently of our God-given dignity and inner freedom. People in the most limiting and terrible of circumstances often demonstrate this truth. We may know of someone, for example, who has been paralyzed from the neck down, powerless to do anything for himself, who chooses not to be angry or bitter but to be grateful for daily blessings and to respond to his caretakers with a gentle spirit. No one has demonstrated this freedom more clearly than Jesus, who, while he was dying a cruel and painful death, forgave those who were crucifying him.[10]

The sense of powerlessness can be debilitating if we succumb to it, but it has the potential for healing if it reminds us that, for every person, life involves both things we can control and things we cannot. *During times of personal grief, it is important to focus on the things still within our power.* The emotion of powerlessness reminds us that we are human beings, not God; yet it also helps us realize that God has given each of us the freedom to decide how we will relate to our situations. As long as we have consciousness, the power of that freedom will never be taken from us. And under most conditions, there are practical actions we can and should take as well.

## Guilt

*Guilt is another emotion many of us have when we become victims of a life-changing loss. When we experience a personal tragedy, we are* prone to ask ourselves very early in the grieving process whether what happened was our fault or whether we might have somehow been able to prevent it.

Even though we cannot think of anything we could have done to change the outcome, we still may have a general sense of guilt. We may be reluctant to think of ourselves as innocent victims, even when reason tells us that we bear no responsibility for what has occurred. *Sometimes those who have survived a tragedy when others died develop what the psychologists call* survivor guilt. *Such people feel guilty not because they believe they were responsible for causing the tragedy but because they survived it and others did not. They feel they did not deserve to survive when those less fortunate perished.*

Misplaced guilt can also impact those who are victims of violence. We are likely to experience such guilt if a loved one has become an addict or committed suicide. And we probably will be burdened with these unwarranted feelings if a relative has carried out an atrocious deed such as a violent crime.

In these and similar cases, progress toward recovery and healing can be delayed for a very long time. When we are consumed with torturing ourselves with what-ifs, accusations, and self-blame, we become emotionally and spiritually paralyzed. Struggling with feelings of guilt when we are not guilty of anything relevant wastes our energy for the legitimate work of negotiating the journey of grief. Even when hindsight reveals something we might have done had we anticipated the outcome, guilt is still unproductive, except perhaps to motivate us and guide us when facing future situations.

But what if we do bear some responsibility for a tragic situation? What if our careless or selfish decisions have resulted in our suffering or the innocent suffering of others? *Just as it is detrimental to feel guilty about things truly beyond our control, it is also unhealthy to avoid accountability for those things for which we are responsible.*

When we truly are guilty, we may choose to play the victim role instead of admitting our wrongs. If we refuse to acknowledge our legitimate guilt, we are unable to undergo the changes necessary for healing. And as long as we fail to accept responsibility for our actions, we are likely to repeat similar behavior in the future, causing additional suffering.

For people of faith, healthy grieving involves sorting out our personal transgressions from uncontrollable circumstances. If we bear responsibility for harming ourselves or others, we must honestly confess our sins and ask God, in faith, for forgiveness. We must pray for the willingness to receive God's mercy and for the courage to seek forgiveness from everyone we have harmed.

If we are honest with ourselves, with God, and with those we have wronged, and if we humbly ask for forgiveness, then nothing we have done is so terrible it cannot be forgiven. Of course, sometimes other people may be unwilling to forgive us. But that is not our responsibility. If we are genuine in our repentance, we can be assured that God *does* forgive us. And experiencing God's forgiveness is the prerequisite for moving on, making amends, righting wrongs, and taking the next steps toward healing.

## Spiritual Work

When we choose to live as victims, we do not look within for solutions. The difficult spiritual work—our share of the healing process—is left undone because we constantly are looking outward for some type of rescue. We might expect to win the lottery or look for someone to suddenly appear and make everything OK again. We wait and hope that such a rescue will take place.

As people of faith, we often pray for God to take away our difficulties. And many of us have at different times received answers to our prayers, whether for ourselves or for others. But what are we to conclude when people of faith experience outcomes other than what they asked for? An entire church earnestly prays for a child injured in an automobile accident, yet she remains in a coma and eventually dies. A family surrounds the bed of a seriously ill man, praying through the night for his recovery, but he does not make it. Such things happen every day.

When their prayers are not answered according to their desires, it is not unusual for misguided people to blame their own weak faith. They have failed to understand the difference between those things that are up to God and the things for which we are responsible. And they have failed to grasp that all prayers need to be offered in the spirit of Jesus' words in the garden of Gethsemane: "Not my will, but yours be done."[11]

When we are in the midst of grief, we do need rescuing, but not necessarily the way we would like. Sometimes help comes in strange forms. It may be an "accidental" meeting or conversation. Other people can be instruments of God in our recovery, even when they are not consciously aware of their role. So can the movies and television programs we watch or the books we read. God is constantly speaking to us, whether we are listening or not, and he will use any means necessary to get our attention and help us negotiate our journeys safely and successfully.

### Andrew's Story

"Mr. Jim and Ms. Jenny" moved into the house next door to Andrew's a little before the boy's eighth birthday. Andrew was disappointed at first. He had hoped his new neighbors would be a family with children near his own age. What he got instead was a gray-haired retired couple.

When he wasn't at school, Andrew was lonely. His mother took him to soccer, but she was too busy with Beth, his baby sister, to play with him. His dad's job required a lot of travel, and when he was home, he was too tired to do anything with his son. Much of Andrew's playtime was centered on his preoccupation with superheroes. He had a collection of superhero comic books, movies, action figures, and costumes. Mr. Jim and Ms. Jenny often watched, as they sat on their porch, while Andrew, wearing one of his colorful outfits, leaped off the ledge of his jungle gym and chased the bad guys through the tunnel and under the slide.

It did not take long for Andrew to change the way he felt about his new neighbors. Ms. Jenny baked cookies and bought treats for Andrew and his little sister, mostly around holidays but sometimes for no reason at all. Mr. Jim was a kind gentleman, and most afternoons Andrew spent some time sitting on the porch, rocking and talking with him. Andrew loved Mr. Jim's stories.

When Andrew was eleven, his mom and dad began to fight a lot. Mr. Jim and Ms. Jenny knew there was trouble next door. They sometimes could hear the yelling and door slamming. At first Andrew did not mention the family problems to Mr. Jim, and though the old gentleman could see the distress on the young boy's face, he did not pry. They talked on the porch each afternoon as if nothing had changed.

But at the large party with family and friends for Andrew's twelfth birthday, an argument broke out between Andrew's mother and the mother of one of the other boys, with angry screaming and sounds of broken glass. Andrew's mom accused one of the other moms of having an affair with Andrew's father. Within minutes, all the visitors retrieved their children and left.

That night, Andrew's parents continued to yell at each other for what seemed like several hours. Each of them, without regard for the ears of the children, accused the other of unspeakable infidelities. Sometime that night, after the children were in bed, Andrew's father packed a bag and left. He would never return.

Andrew's father rented his own apartment, and the woman his mother had argued with at the birthday party left her family within days and moved in with him. For as long as Andrew could remember, his father had been gone more than he was home. Now he was gone all the time. Soon Andrew's mother had a houseguest of her own, someone she brought home one night after a date. The man stayed that night and never left.

In a few short weeks, Andrew's universe had been turned upside down, and he was seriously depressed. When his parents had started fighting, Andrew prayed nightly for God to make them stop. They didn't. When his father left, Andrew prayed for his father to come home and for his parents to reconcile. They didn't.

Andrew began to talk with Mr. Jim about what was happening. Mr. Jim listened quietly and sympathetically. Andrew felt it was good to have someone to tell his troubles to. "I thought God was supposed to answer prayers. He sure didn't answer mine."

"You think God isn't answering your prayers?" Mr. Jim asked softly.

"I have prayed over and over for God to make my mom and dad love each other again and to get back together. It's like God doesn't hear me or care. I think maybe this stuff about God is like the Santa Claus thing," Andrew said with a frown. "Maybe it's just a story grown-ups tell. Maybe there isn't a God, and that's why he doesn't answer my prayers."

"Well, Andrew," Mr. Jim said, "I see you have started asking some of the really tough questions. Do you think it is possible God does answer our prayers but not always the way we want him to?"

"What do you mean?"

"Well, take that Santa Claus thing you mentioned. Can you remember a time when you didn't get what you asked Santa Claus to bring?"

"I don't think so."

"Why do you think that is? Do you think maybe your mom and dad made sure you didn't ask Santa for something they couldn't afford or something they didn't want you to have because it would not be good for you?"

"I guess so."

"The Santa thing is a made-up story," Mr. Jim continued, "but your mother and father are real. So is their love for you, no matter what it feels like now. They always wanted you to have a happy Christmas and didn't want you to be disappointed. But they also did not want you to have a present that would be dangerous or not good for you. You were too young to know what was best for you, so they made sure you got only things that were OK for you to have. I bet there were a lot of other times that you wanted to buy something or do something and they said no. Am I right?"

"Oh yeah! They said no a lot of times."

"Do you think they were just being mean?"

After a thoughtful moment, Andrew answered, "No, I think they were trying to be good parents. But what I don't understand is, if they really love me, why is my mom living with someone besides my dad, and why did my dad have to leave? And if he still loves me, why doesn't he call?"

"I don't know either, Andrew. I think that is wrong of him, and the whole thing is a mess. But here's what I believe. I believe God isn't going to make your parents do the right thing, no matter how much you pray for it. God doesn't work like that. God gives people the power of choice and doesn't take that away even when their choices are bad. I also believe that God loves you and wants what is best for you. And I believe God still loves and takes care of us, even when it feels like we are getting a bad deal. And somehow, God will make sure, if we trust him, that what we get in this life are the blessings he wants us to have. They may not be the particular blessings we asked for, and sometimes they may not look like blessings at first, but they will be exactly what we need."

"But don't you think God wants my mom and dad to get back together?"

"That's a tough one. I honestly don't know. But I wonder at this point if the relationship between your parents is so broken that if they did get back together, it would be worse for everyone than the way it is now. It is really tough to live in a house with parents who don't love each other anymore. But I also know that having your father abandon you is probably the most painful thing a young man can experience."

A week later, Mr. Jim and Andrew sat rocking silently on the porch watching a hummingbird drink from the flowers in the pots by the steps. "Did I ever tell you about the time my dad left me?" Mr. Jim asked.

"Your dad left *you*?"

"It was different from the way your dad left," Mr. Jim continued, "but he did leave me. And I don't think I ever quite got over it. It happened back in the Korean War. My dad was in the army in World War II, and after the war he joined the Army Reserves. When the Korean War broke out, they called him back. I was thirteen at the time, and I'll never forget standing at the train station shaking hands with him and telling him good-bye. I tried not to cry, but I didn't quite succeed. The last thing Dad said to me before he got on the train was, 'You're the man of the house now. You take care of your mother and sister.' I waved to him as the train pulled out of the station. He waved back. It was the last time I ever saw him. He was killed in action a few months later."

"I bet you were really sad when that happened."

"I was. And I had a hard time, just like you are having now, because I prayed so hard for Dad to be safe and come home, and he never did." After another long silence, Mr. Jim said, "I think I already told you that when I was young, I had a big collection of comic books."

"Yep. And you said almost all of them were about superheroes."

"That's right. And do you know what I did after my dad was killed? I gathered all of those comic books. I put them in a big metal oil drum in my backyard and burned every one of them."

"Why did you do that? Do you know how much money they would be worth today?"

"Probably a lot, Andrew. But I needed to burn them because it was time for me to grow up. I think until my dad died, I believed in my heart that if I was a good boy and something really bad was about to happen, some superhero would swoop down and save the day. I think just about everyone wants that—a superhero to rescue us from all of life's troubles. Don't get me wrong, Andrew. Just about every society that ever has existed has had stories about superheroes. They entertain us. They inspire us to struggle against the evil in this world. They teach us about honesty, justice, courage, and self-sacrifice for the good of others. But the time comes when we need to leave the world of superheroes behind."

"Because they are not real?" Andrew interjected.

"Yes, because they are not real, and because our lives and problems *are* real, and we need to face them and deal with them without the fantasy that someone else is going to magically fix our problems."

"But isn't that why we pray? Aren't we asking God to fix our problems?"

"You sure do ask some good questions, Andrew. OK. Here is how I think it works. Sometimes when we ask God to do something, God says yes, and we get what we ask for. There are boys and girls who have prayed for their parents to get back together, and sure enough they did, though not necessarily as soon as the children would have liked. At other times God says no. There are many boys and girls who have prayed for their parents to get back together and it did not happen."

"Is that because some kids are good and some are bad?"

"Oh no! That has nothing to do with it. God loves all of his children and wants them all to have good things."

"Then why do we bother to pray?"

"That is another very good question, Andrew. I think God is happy for us to ask for the things we want. But God is not Santa Claus or our magical genie. God is there to strengthen and guide us through the journey of life. Sometimes what we want is for God to make our situation better. But what God wants is for us to grow in our capacity to deal with our troubles and to grow in faith. So instead of giving us an improved situation, God offers us the chance to be stronger as a person and in our faith.

"At some point along the way, Andrew," Mr. Jim went on, "the time comes when we must learn how to pray adult prayers. When we grow up in our relationship with God, prayer is no longer about getting God to make our lives be the way we want them to be. It is about having our lives be the way God wants them to be."

Andrew thought a lot about that conversation with Mr. Jim over the next several days. He was not ready to burn his collection of superhero movies, costumes, and souvenirs—yet. But he did box them up and put them in the attic. And Andrew did try to ask God to help him the way Mr. Jim had suggested.

The next few years were not smooth sailing for Andrew by any means. He remained estranged from his father. He didn't always get along with his step dad. He sometimes got into trouble for not doing what he was supposed to do. But his teen years could have been much worse. With Mr. Jim's encouragement, he joined a church youth group, and in that group he found a kind of second family. With the help of his friends in the group and the church's counselors, Andrew grew in his faith and in his desire to know and do God's will. He was always one of the first ones in the group to volunteer for mission trips and service projects.

When Andrew went off to college, he joined and soon became a leader in the campus Christian movement. During his sophomore year, he was asked to speak at one of the annual Christian rallies for high-school-age youth, similar to the ones he once had attended with his own youth group.

Looking out on several hundred young people attending the rally that Saturday morning, Andrew told them of the important role Mr. Jim had played in his life after his father and mother separated and then divorced. "What I wanted at the time was for God to send me a superhero to fix things the way I thought they should be fixed. But as you may have noticed, there never seems to be a superhero around when you really need one."

Andrew noticed nods and smiles in the audience.

"Instead," he continued, "God sent me a real-life hero in the form of a gray-haired older man who moved into the house next door. We had many talks about life and about God over the years. With a gentle hand, Mr. Jim pointed me to Jesus Christ. Without those talks, I know I would have become a very different person.

"One day, when I was fourteen, I saw Mr. Jim sitting on the front porch whittling. I had seen him doing that before. I couldn't believe how good he was at carving animals. I went over and asked Mr. Jim if he could teach me to carve an animal. Mr. Jim agreed to teach me, only after he first showed me how to work the knife so as not to cut myself.

"Once the safety lesson was done, Mr. Jim said I should start by carving a bear out of a block of wood. 'If you can carve a bear,' he said, 'you can carve about anything.' So he fetched a block of basswood from his workshop, handed it to me, and told me to make a bear.

"'But how do I get started. How do I make a bear?' I asked.

"'It is real simple' he responded. 'You just take a block of wood and you whittle away everything that is not a bear.'

"'You make it sound easy. It can't be that easy,' I protested.

"'I didn't say it was easy,' he responded. 'I said it was simple.' Then he patiently showed me how to outline the bear on the block of wood, and I began whittling away everything that was not a bear.

"Mr. Jim is in heaven now. He passed away about a year ago. But as I have thought about my journey with him, I have realized how much life is like carving that bear. We show up in life with a lot of potential, potential that can be shaped for good or for evil. God has in mind what he wants us to become, just like I knew I wanted that block of wood to become a bear. Our job, with God's help, is to carve away everything that is not what God wants us to be.

"One of the things God has helped me whittle away is the child in me who fantasized about superheroes coming to rescue me from my troubles. Mr. Jim introduced me to a different kind of hero. Because of Mr. Jim, I have come to know Jesus. Through God's amazing grace, I now experience Jesus in my spiritual heart. It is Jesus, the hero within me, who strengthens me when I am challenged by life's circumstances. And it is Jesus who whittles at my imperfections and leads me on my journey."

Not long after that speech, Andrew visited Mr. Jim's grave. On the tombstone he placed a beautifully carved bear.

### Your Story

1. Read 2 Corinthians 12:8–9. Have you ever pleaded with God to take away some difficulty? Can you think of any difficulties in your life that have been removed? Is there a difficulty in your life that has not been taken away?

2. What does, "My grace is sufficient for you, for my power is made perfect in weakness," mean to you when you must face the reality that a difficulty has not and will not be taken away?

3. Have you ever been tempted to live like a victim of your problems? How is choosing the victim role a form of unfaith?

4. Read Luke 22:42. What do you think is the difference between childish prayers and grown-up prayers? What grown-up prayer do you need to pray today?

5. Can you describe an experience in your life when God's Spirit within you guided you in doing something that you do not think you could have done on your own?

## STEP 3

# RESIST THE TEMPTATION TO GET STUCK

When we allow ourselves to become stuck in one or more of the stages of grief, we delay healing or prevent it altogether. With God's help we can resist the temptation to persist in questioning, anger, and depression and become free to continue the journey toward recovery.

*The LORD answered Job out of the storm. He said:*
*"Who is this that darkens my counsel*
*with words without knowledge?*
*Brace yourself like a man;*
*I will question you,*
*and you shall answer me."*

JOB 38:1–3

*The LORD said to Cain, "Why are you angry?"*

GENESIS 4:6

*When he rose from prayer and went back to the disciples, he*
*found them asleep, exhausted from sorrow. "Why are you*
*sleeping?" he asked them. "Get up and pray so that you will*
*not fall into temptation."*

LUKE 22:45–46

*God is faithful; he will not let you be tempted beyond what*
*you can bear. But when you are tempted,*
*he will also provide a way out so that you can*
*stand up under it.*

1 CORINTHIANS 10:13

6

# QUESTIONING
### Why Do You Keep Asking Why?

*My God, my God, why have you forsaken me? Why are you so
far from saving me, so far from the words of my groaning?*
PSALM 22:1

In times of grief, we tend to ask a lot of questions. When we are in *shock* and *denial*, we ask, "Is this really happening? Is there a way for it not to be true?" When we are trying to avoid facing the reality of our losses through some form of *escape*, we want to know, "Where can I flee? Where is a safe place?" If we are in the *victim* role, we wonder, "Who is going to rescue me? When is it going to happen?"

At some point in our journeys of grief, most of us reach the place where it is no longer possible to live in denial, avoidance, or false hope. The reality of our situations breaks through our defenses, and we are compelled to face the truth of what has happened, no matter how difficult. To the question of whether a personal tragedy is real, we must answer yes. To the question of where we can flee to safety, we are forced to answer, "Nowhere." To the questions about who or what will come to give us a different situation and when that will take place, we are required to admit, "It's not going to happen."

At the point when it is no longer possible to avoid facing the reality of our losses and their implications, we often find ourselves uttering a new question: Why?

## The Why Question

*Why* may be the most asked of all human questions, because we want to believe there is an explanation for everything. Sometimes when we ask why, we actually mean *how*, as in questions of why things in the physical universe work the way they do. For example, if we ask why hurricanes form over the ocean, we probably are expecting a meteorological explanation. On the other hand, when a hurricane strikes our community, causing loss of life and property, the why question seldom is about cause and effect. Or if a loved one dies in a car accident and we ask why, we usually are not looking for an explanation about someone running a light or passing on a curve. We are seeking something much more profound.

When we ask why in the midst of tragedy, we most often are asking a spiritual question, whether or not we recognize it to be so. *Why* questions tend to arise when we no longer can avoid facing the reality of our situations and we long to reach a place on our journey where we again will have some serenity. When we ask why, we are expressing a desire to reach acceptance, to make peace with our situation, and to find some spiritual solace. But the question itself is a sign that we are not yet ready to embrace the reality of our losses. Before we can know acceptance, we must continue awhile on the journey of grief. We have more work to do.

We all want to believe that things happen in this world for a reason. We sometimes imagine that if someone could answer the question why to our personal satisfaction, we might be able to make our peace with what has happened. This is particularly true of people of faith. We may feel we have seen God's mysterious hand working for good in all sorts of situations. But at the moment of being no longer able to avoid coming to terms with our losses, we are unable to see any point to such things. We find ourselves questioning God's justice and love. Such feelings are normal, though we may not feel they are.

While asking why is perfectly natural, the difficulty is that no explanation will satisfy us. If someone tells us, "God does not make such things happen," we want to know *why* God made a universe where such stuff happens anyway. If we are counseled that this is a part of God's plan, then we want to know *why* a good God would make such an awful plan. If someone attempts to explain to us why there is evil in the world, we ask them why innocent victims must suffer for the sins of others. Every explanation results in another why question.

## Why Me?

One reason the answers we receive seem inadequate is that we are asking a profoundly personal question. When I found myself asking why after the onset of my son's mental illness, I was not just asking why such things happen in the universe but why this terrible thing had happened to me and to someone I love. Why me? is a question that arises out of what usually are hidden assumptions about our lives in this world.

At some level of our being, we believe that bad stuff happens to *other* people. We see it on the news every night. We consider this reality to be regrettable but expected. We may wonder why such awful things happen to innocent people in this world, but rarely do we lose sleep over it. Sometimes particular events make us especially sad and create within us a desire to help relieve the suffering of those who have experienced some terrible loss. Yet whether we become involved in their suffering is entirely optional.

But it is a different matter when a tragedy impacts us personally. At some level, we think terrible things may happen to others, but they are not supposed to happen to *us*. Perhaps this is because at some dimension of our consciousness, we think of ourselves as special and therefore exempt from tragedy. Or maybe it is because we cling to the notion that bad things happen only to bad people, while those who live good lives are immune from such things. And if we are persons of faith, we may make the assumption that "a good and faithful servant" will be protected by God at all times from all but the smallest of troubles. So when tragedy strikes us, we cry out not only about why it is happening but also why it is happening *to us*.

None of this is to say it is wrong for us to ask *why* questions. For many of us, healing can come only when we have struggled with these questions of the heart. But if we are to continue successfully on our journey, it is important to remember that we seek something deeper than explanations.

## A Sign of Anguish

When I was a young pastor, I attempted to comfort the parents of a sweet little girl who had died of a kidney disease by giving them theological explanations about why bad things happen to good people. When the couple remained inconsolable, I felt like a failure. It was not until some time later, after I had experienced the death of a good friend, that I realized how insensitive and irrelevant my words had been. I had been so focused on defending God that I failed to be present to the depth of the suffering of those parents.

As Jesus was dying on the cross, he quoted Psalm 22:1. He cried out to his heavenly Father, "My God, my God, why have you forsaken me?"[12] It should be clear to all thoughtful readers of Scripture that Jesus was not asking a philosophical question about his suffering. He was expressing to God the Father his anguish and feeling of abandonment, the feeling we all have when we are alone in our agony. Clearly we need not be concerned that God is in any way offended by our questioning. Those who ask why can take comfort in knowing that both the psalmist and Jesus asked the question during their own most personal tragedies.

Therefore, while the question, why me? may be for us an indication of a misplaced notion of entitlement in this world, it also should be understood as a cry of the heart. It is a calling out to our Creator to hear our distress. It is a means of letting God know how much pain we are in. Just as children feel the need to let parents know how much they hurt after falling down and scraping their knees, so we too have a mysterious need to express to God the anguish of our emotional pain. And that should be recognized as a clue to the function of the questioning phase in the healing process. When we can be honest with ourselves about the reality of our losses, and when we can be honest with God about the degree of our pain, we are preparing ourselves for healing.

## God's Questions of Us

Much of the book of Job deals with the questions raised by a good and righteous man who experienced unimaginable losses. Job asked God, "Why did I not die in my mother's womb? Why have you made me a target? Why do I struggle in vain?"[13]

Toward the end of the account, God turns the tables on Job. Up until then, God has listened patiently to Job's lament. But now God commands Job, "Brace yourself like a man; I will question you, and you shall answer me." What follows is a series of questions designed to make the point that Job, a human being, is not in a position to understand the ways of the Lord of heaven and earth.

When we find ourselves struggling with why? and why me?, it is helpful for us also to listen for the questions God is asking *us*. God can handle our questions just fine. Asking them can help prepare us for the next step of our journey. But we are not likely to take that step successfully if we do not cease our questioning of God long enough to hear him question us.

For example, we may sense that God is asking us, "What attitude are you going to have about your loss? Are you going to be bitter and angry? Are you going to give in to depression and give up? What are you going to do?" Or we may feel ourselves being asked, "When are you going to notice the many ways I am caring for you in your grief?" and "How can this emotionally painful change in your life help you to become a kinder, more loving person?" With such questions, God calls us away from the seduction of self-pity and the temptation to live our lives as a protest against the way life is for all of us.

## Cynthia's Story

From the moment they met, Cynthia and Mike both believed they were soul mates. That conviction had become even stronger over their twenty-six-year marriage. They loved to share experiences, and they cherished every moment when they could be alone together. When their youngest daughter finally went off to college, they celebrated their new opportunity for intimacy and freedom with a second honeymoon on a Caribbean cruise. A few weeks later, forty-eight-year-old Mike dropped dead of a heart attack while jogging in the park early one Saturday morning. Cynthia felt as if everything that made her life worth living had been destroyed.

Once the initial shock had eased and her denial had worn thin, the forty-seven-year-old widow became obsessed with a question she could neither answer nor avoid. "Why?" she tearfully asked over and over. "Why did this happen to me?" she asked night after night, as she lay sleepless and alone in her bed. It was the only prayer she was able to pray. She tried to pray the types of prayers she thought people were supposed to pray in similar situations, prayers for comfort and strength to face her difficulties. But she could never finish those prayers. In midsentence she would fill with anguish, and the only words that came were the lone words that expressed how she truly felt. "Why, God? Why me?" No answer came

Cynthia and Mike had built their marriage and family life on faith. There was never any question about how the family would spend Sundays. They all went to Sunday school and church, and when the children were old enough, they went to the youth group on Sunday evenings as well. For many years the couple hosted a small-group Bible study in their home, and they practiced a serious though sporadic devotional life. The family prayed together at mealtime, and both parents had been conscientious about helping the children deal with life challenges in the context of faith.

Still, Cynthia always had a rather simple faith, uncomplicated by serious doubts or questions. She knew, as everyone does, that life can bring sudden and unexpected tragedy. But she never really believed it could happen to her. Cynthia would not have admitted it, but deep inside, she believed that because she, Mike, and the children were a Christian family, God had placed some kind of protective shield around them. As far back as she could remember, she had thought that if she did her part, God would protect her and those close to her from harm. Intellectually she knew better, but in her heart of hearts, she was convinced that as long as she was not a bad person, bad things would not happen to her. At least, she had believed that until Mike died. Now she did not know what to believe.

For a long time, Cynthia did not tell anyone about her spiritual struggle. It occurred to her that she might speak with a friend or her pastor about her questioning. She played out the scenario in her mind but soon rejected the idea as too risky. She decided neither of them would understand what she was going through. She would get no satisfying answers, she predicted, only painful feelings of being judged for what she already had come to believe was her inadequate faith. Cynthia continued to ask why night after night and chose to suffer alone.

One weekend when Cynthia's three-year-old grandson was visiting her, she found herself irritated because the child was asking her why about almost everything. And when she answered as best she could, he would again ask, "Why?"

Toward the end of the weekend, she turned the table on him. "Why do you ask why so much?" she asked him.

He frowned, stuck out his bottom lip in a pout, and in a rather pitiful voice said, "I don't know."

"Well, I will tell you a secret," Cynthia said softly. "Sometimes when you ask why, I don't know either." Needless to say, only a few minutes passed before she was bombarded by another series of questions.

Cynthia doubted that a three-year-old was capable of the kind of reflection she was demanding with her challenge to him. But she thought a person of her own mature years certainly ought to be. So, she asked herself, *why is it that I keep asking why?*

Cynthia had been struggling alone with her questioning for several weeks when Ruth, an old college friend Cynthia had not thought about in years, called to express condolences. Ruth told Cynthia she had heard from a mutual acquaintance about Mike's death. She had lost her own husband, Tom, to pancreatic cancer almost two years earlier. She suggested that the two of them get together to renew their friendship, and Cynthia eagerly accepted the offer.

After the two widows shared their accounts of loss and talked about the differences in impact between a sudden death and a slow dying, Cynthia shared with Ruth her obsession with the question why.

"So you are a *why baby* too," Ruth said. "I certainly know where you are coming from. You have lots of company. Been there, done that."

"So what's the answer?" Cynthia asked. "I need someone to please tell me why this happened to me. Why did Mike have to die?"

"Let me ask you something," Ruth responded gently. "What kind of answer are you looking for?

"What do you mean?"

"Well, do you think it would help if someone explained to you what caused his heart attack?"

"Of course not. I know all that. The doctor told me all about the blockage and how it killed him. That's not what I'm asking."

"I was fairly sure it wasn't. So what kind of answer do you want?"

"I suppose one that will make sense out of what happened. I just don't know what it would be."

"Exactly. Can you think of any response to your question that would satisfy you or take away your pain?"

"I'm not sure what you mean."

"After Tom got sick and we knew he was going to die, people saw I was struggling and tried to comfort me. They said things like, 'It is God's will,' or, 'Things happen for a reason,' which may be true in some unfathomable way, but their answers just irritated me and caused me to ask more questions."

"I know. When people say those things to me, I want to come back with 'Why is it God's will? What possible reason could he have?' Of course, I don't say that. I just smile and thank them."

"Until people have been through something similar, Cynthia, I don't think they are capable of understanding that we don't really want their explanations."

"But if we don't want answers, why do we keep asking why? What do we really want?"

"I know what I wanted when my Tom died. I would have given anything to be able to turn back the clock and restore things to the way they used to be, the way things were for us before he got sick. We had a wonderful, happy life together."

Cynthia's eyes began to water. "That's what I want too. Some nights I cry myself to sleep, wishing I could have him back for just one more day."

Ruth retrieved a tissue from her purse and offered it to her friend. "It's hard, I know. It feels so final. We want things to go back to the way they were, but we know in our hearts that life doesn't work that way."

The sandwich shop had now become crowded and noisy. Cynthia and Ruth decided to take a walk around a small lake in a nearby park.

Once there, Cynthia restarted the conversation. "So if an answer isn't what I really want, why can't I stop asking why?"

"As I've thought about my own journey with Tom's illness and death and all the time I spent stuck in my questioning phase, I've realized something about myself. I think that when I was asking God all those questions, I wanted God to know how much I was hurting. I felt some great cosmic mistake has been made, and I couldn't fix it. All I could do was express the pain I was in."

"Now that you say it, that's exactly where I think I am right now. But you don't seem to be stuck anymore. How did you get past it?"

Ruth paused for a moment before responding. "After my Tom passed away, I went into a serious state of self-pity. Then, after many months of asking, why me? it hit me: Why *not* me? We live in a world where a lot of bad stuff goes down every day. Did I have any more right to a life free of tragedy than anyone else? What kind of narcissistic pride is that? Jesus said the rain falls on both the just and the unjust,[14] and I take that to mean it does so whether it is a gentle rain needed for crops to grow or a terrible destructive flood. It isn't personal, even though it affects me very personally."

The two continued on the path by the lake until they found a bench facing the water.

"I also had another insight along the way," Ruth reflected. "When everything was going great, I didn't think to ask, why me? I only did that after it all was taken from me. The whole time Tom and I were together, I took our wonderful life for granted. I don't think I appreciated all those precious moments we had together. But after they were gone, I sure grieved their loss. It has taken a lot of time. But I now thank God for the wonderful times we shared. I realize today that I grieved so greatly because I loved and was loved so much. How blessed I am to have had such a wonderful marriage. Now, I try each day to appreciate the important relationships in life I still have."

"We had wonderful times too. I miss him. I really, really miss him."

"Of course you do. And I miss Tom with all my being. I still don't know why Tom was taken from me, and I don't know why Mike was taken from you. And I'm fairly certain that neither does anybody else except God; and sometimes, in my weaker moments, I am not so sure about God. All I know is, if we weren't confronted by a mystery, we would not need to ask why. We are experiencing the mysterious nature of life and of God. We want to take the mystery out of the mystery, but there is no way to do that."

"So does that mean you have stopped asking why?"

"To be perfectly honest, not entirely. But I have done a lot of praying for the ability to accept the things in life over which I have no control. And while my cries of 'Why?' have gone unanswered with regard to explanations, they have been answered in other ways. God has helped me make progress in coming to terms with Tom's death. So I continue to pray for guidance and direction, and I feel that is starting to happen. In fact, I think that is why I called you. When I heard about your loss, I had the strongest feeling that I should get together with you."

A little more than a year later, Cynthia was asked to teach her adult Sunday school class. When she discovered the lesson was to be about the Old Testament character Job, whose family and wealth were taken from him in sudden tragedy, she smiled and thought, *God has quite a sense of humor.*[15]

Cynthia told the story of her journey, her questioning, and her conversation with Ruth. "When Mike died, it overwhelmed me. I was disoriented. Before it happened, life made sense. Afterwards, all my beliefs were called into question. I couldn't understand why God let it happen. Sometimes I wonder whether I would have become stuck in a state of questioning for the rest of my days if God had not put Ruth in my life.

"I lost my husband. Job lost his entire family along with everything else that belonged to him. He was God's faithful servant, and horrible things happened to him. The devastating losses threw him into a crisis of faith. The Bible makes it clear that Job was a person desperately attempting to hold on to an inadequate faith that failed to account for the reality of his real-life experience. Whatever his sin, Job knew his suffering was exceedingly out of proportion to the events that had befallen him. He said, 'If I have sinned, what have I done to you, O watcher of men? Why have you made me your target? Have I become a burden to you?' (Job 7:20).

"Job was broken by the weight of his losses. His tragedy was too great to fit into his old theology. He was forced to question all his assumptions about life and faith. He begged God to put him out of his misery and just let him die, and when that didn't happen, he dared to question God's wisdom and justice. In the great climax of that drama, God turned the tables. God questioned Job for assuming the creature could understand, question, and judge the Creator of all that is. And Job learned, as countless others have learned, that after tragedy strikes, nothing is ever the same again. But there can be a new beginning.

"I now know that when I kept asking, why me? I was longing for healing. When we understand that our deepest desire is for God to acknowledge our devastation, we are able to transform our questioning into a prayer for healing. And when we begin to seek healing, we are on our way to recovery, which will benefit not only us but also those around us who need us to be there for *them* in times of difficulty. That is what happened to my friend Ruth. And because she had made that journey, it has happened to me as well. Ruth and I never found answers to our questions of why our life mates were taken from us so early. But we have experienced something else that we have come to believe is far more beneficial: *'O Lᴏʀᴅ my God, I called to you for help and you healed me'"* (Ps. 30:2).

———————————— *Your Story* ————————————

1.  Read Psalm 22:1 and Mark 15:34. Have you ever felt like crying out, "My God, my God, why have you forsaken me?" If so, what were you going through at the time?
2.  Do you think being a Christian and living a moral and compassionate life should protect you from suffering? How fairly do you think suffering is distributed in this world?
3.  Why do you think we tend to ask, why me? when we experience loss but not when we experience blessings?
4.  Read Job 38:1–3. God questioned Job. Have you ever experienced God questioning you? What questions do you think he may be asking you today?
5.  If God were to call you by name and ask you, "What now? What are you going to do with your life?" what do you think you would say?

# 7

# ANGER
## Who Pushed Humpty Dumpty?

*Ask the animals, and they will teach you,*
*or the birds of the air, and they will tell you;*
*or speak to the earth, and it will teach you,*
*or let the fish of the sea inform you.*
*Which of all these does not know*
*that the hand of the* LORD *has done this?*

JOB 12:7–9

Asking, why? and why me? often arises from the feeling that a terrible personal loss was not fair. When this perception persists and we remain unwilling to accept the reality of what has happened, we may attempt to place blame, and we enter a time of anger.

For the most part, people are unlikely to become angry when their losses conform to their expectations about the natural patterns of life. When we lose a parent who has reached a normal life expectancy, sorrow may be profound, but it probably will not be accompanied by anger. And when a loved one has gone through much suffering and death finally comes, we are much more inclined to feel relief rather than anger.

On the other hand, anger is a very common reaction when people die long before their expected times. When disease takes a young child's life or a teenager drowns, feelings of anger are to be expected. We are also prone to anger when careless, selfish, and irresponsible actions have brought about our loss. Grief over the infidelity of a mate usually manifests itself as anger. And almost always we will react with anger if our personal tragedy has resulted from a malicious act such as a terrorist attack, a rape, or a murder.

Such diverse circumstances can explain why an individual who has experienced several seasons of grief over the years may have become angry during some of them but not during others. If we have successfully negotiated periods of anger during earlier seasons of grief, we also may find we are less likely to become angry when facing losses later in life. Yet even then, some types of tragedies are likely to trigger an anger response.

We have observed in earlier chapters that denial, escape, victimism, and questioning can have positive benefits. We also have recognized that they carry with them temptations and great risks. The same can be said for anger.

## The Gift of Anger

Anger is a powerful emotion intended by God for the well-being of the human family. As the sound of a rattler warns an intruder not to step on a venomous snake, so expressions of anger can have positive results. They may tell those who might do us harm that we will not easily be victimized. They may remind would-be bullies and predators to consider the possible consequences their actions might bring upon themselves.

Among many of God's creatures, when a threat is encountered, anger transforms fear into courage. Anger gives strength to the weak and at times makes possible the defeat of a more powerful enemy. Ordinary people in frightening situations can become heroes because of their anger. A regular foot soldier filled with fury by the death of a buddy at the hands of an enemy has been known to lead an attack and turn the tide of battle. Or think of a petite woman who becomes possessed by rage and successfully fights off her much larger attacker.

Anger motivates. It is a potent weapon for challenging injustice and righting wrongs. The Old Testament prophets angrily denounced the unfaithfulness and wrongdoing of the people of Israel. When Jesus saw the money changers in the temple, he drove them out in what appears to have been a state of righteous anger.[16]

When my son first became ill, I did not know much about the treatments available for people with schizophrenia. During the first couple of years, I received a disturbing education. Most private mental health practitioners were not interested in serving people with his diagnosis. They much preferred to work with otherwise healthy clients who were trying to deal with everyday problems of living. The primary service available for my son was hospitalization, but unless he was willing to admit himself, it was for the most part an impractical option. A common symptom of schizophrenia is the person's failure to recognize his or her need for treatment. Moreover, at the time, the legal requirements for involuntary admission required a patient to have been overtly dangerous to self or others in the previous twenty-four hours. On many occasions, I tried to admit my son for treatment only to be turned away because he would not agree and did not fully meet the criteria for involuntary admission.

I soon learned there were mentally ill young people all over the country who were homeless and wandering the streets in psychotic states because the system of care was broken. Not only was it next to impossible to access hospital care, but there were virtually no relevant community-based services available either.

The more I learned about the problem, the angrier I became. In time, God took that anger and turned it into a passion for change. And the passion would drive me to spend more than a quarter century of my life working toward mental health reform. *When we are grieving a loss, anger can motivate us to transcend self-pity, to abandon the victim role, and to take much-needed actions.* As we will see more fully in chapter 10, angry feelings are sometimes the impetus for activism that addresses serious problems and a stimulus for efforts to help others avoid similar suffering.

### A Dangerous Emotion

While sometimes it may be a good thing, *there is not a more dangerous emotion than anger.* It is a wild force within us that must be tamed and guided before it can be helpful; otherwise it may have terrible consequences for ourselves, for others, and for faith. The danger becomes real when our anger controls us rather than being controlled by us. And the longer we remain stuck in an angry state of mind, the more dangerous our anger becomes.

Psychologists tell us that anger is a basic human emotion. It can be triggered spontaneously when we are confronted by a challenging situation. This often happens when something or someone prevents us from realizing a desire. This automatic response sends chemicals throughout our bodies, prompting us briefly to lose our tempers. But if this response lasts more than a minute or two, it is because we have decided to continue to be angry. When we feel these rushes of anger, we have a choice: we can allow them to continue and thereby release more anger chemicals into our systems, or we can decide to allow these spontaneous responses to melt away. If we do so, the flush of anger will subside within a few moments.

But if we allow it to continue unabated, anger can be like an evil spirit that possesses us, stresses us, and destroys us from within. It can be destructive to our health. It can blind us so that we cannot see the beauty and goodness of the world. It can turn us into bitter and joyless people.

*Anger often destroys relationships, because anger and love cannot long coexist within us.* Anger can stand in the way of the forgiveness and the reconciliation necessary for healing. It can block us from the peace God wants to restore in our hearts. As long as we continue angrily blaming ourselves, blaming others, and blaming God for the occasions of our grief, we will not be able to succeed on our journeys toward recovery.

### "Why Are You Angry?"

In the biblical narrative of Cain and Abel, we are told that each of the brothers offered a sacrifice to God. Abel's sacrifice pleased God, but Cain's did not. The text tells us their offerings were different but not how Cain came to know that his sacrifice was unacceptable. Perhaps Cain expected his sacrifice to result in some kind of personal benefit, and he observed Abel receiving this reward. We do not know. But it is clear from the story that Cain became very angry and downcast. I believe Cain reacted with anger and pouting because he felt God had treated him unfairly.

Neither blessings nor sufferings appear to be handed out in this world in a fair fashion; some lives are much more filled with tragedy and pain than others. We have difficulty understanding why those who do evil may prosper and those who do good may suffer. And we not only ask *why* life is this way, but sometimes we respond, as Cain responded, by becoming angry.

*The unfairness of life may be especially felt when tragedy strikes in a life of faith.* Whatever the reasons for our difficulties, we may feel, as Cain did, that the sacrifices we have made have been in vain. And after suffering major losses, we too may respond with anger and pouting, as we did when we were children and felt we had been treated unfairly. Sometimes, just as Cain became angry with his brother, we may direct our anger toward other children of God. For example, a couple who lose a child to disease may become angry and resentful toward one another, though neither is to blame.

God asked Cain, "Why are you angry? Why are you downcast?" If we pay attention, when we find ourselves angry and pouting, we will hear God asking us those same questions: "Why are you angry? Why are you so upset?" Is it because we feel life has been unfair to us? Do we blame God because we feel we are being unjustly punished? Do we feel someone else needs to be punished so we might feel better? Or do we blame ourselves and feel we deserve to be punished?

Instead of reflecting on God's questions and allowing them to change his attitude, Cain aimed his anger at Abel and killed him. No matter how we answer these questions, we are reminded by this story that great danger accompanies the emotion of anger. When we sense God asking us why we are angry, we need to understand that such a moment is an opportunity to grow spiritually and to take the next step on our journey of grief and faith.

## Overcoming Anger

It is clear, then, that anger can be a powerful emotion threatening to consume us, as wild flames can threaten to consume a house. But how does a person fight the flames of anger?

*The first step is to become willing to let our anger go.* That sounds easier than it is, because we may have become seriously attached to our anger. Angry feelings are addictive. We cling to them the same way we persist in bad habits that threaten our health. We tend to gain a perverse enjoyment from them. *The second step is to recognize that we need God's help in order to extinguish the flames of anger.*

Our first prayer must be for the willingness to let it go, to be free of all resentment toward *ourselves,* toward *others,* and toward *God.* Then when God has made us willing, we need to ask him to remove our anger so we can continue on our journey toward a life beyond grief.

## Carlos's Story

The high school memorial service was a well-attended tribute to a popular young man. Juan, a sixteen-year-old honor student, died when the speeding car in which he was riding ran off the road and flipped into a tree. Juan's parents, Carlos and Maria, though brokenhearted, were justly proud. Nearly everyone in the community had paid their respects in one way or another, and it was obvious that their neighbors and friends grieved their loss with them.

It was not long, however, before Carlos's pride in his son had turned into anger. Carlos was consumed with an indignant sense of the injustice of what had happened. He felt a compelling desire to blame whoever was responsible.

At first, Carlos decided he himself was to blame. He became obsessed with his own transgressions over the years. He had gone to church far less frequently than Maria. He thought about how in his younger years he had been prone to many of the vices God despises. And now, as a middle-aged man, he sometimes lusted, cursed, and drank too much. *Surely,* he thought, *God is punishing me for my sins.*

For several months, Carlos tortured himself with a series of what-ifs. "What if I had been a better man, a better father, a better husband? What if I had spent more time with Juan, or had been stricter with him, like my father was with me?" He wasn't sure what he possibly could have done differently. But Carlos became so angry with himself that he put his fist through the plasterboard wall of his kitchen—a dramatic gesture, but it did not put an end to the questions. "What if I had said no when Juan asked if he could ride in his friend's car to the game? What if I had driven him myself instead of staying home to watch television?" Carlos secretly had been glad he did not have to drive Juan to the game that night. Now he hated himself for it.

Maria tried to assure Carlos that the death was not his fault. But instead of being reassured, Carlos became angrier. He turned on Maria and began to make her the focus of his wrath. It was not that Carlos believed Maria had contributed directly to their son's death; it was just that she was there. He began to yell at her about the smallest matters. Maria was not the kind of woman to let such behavior pass. She was skilled at giving back what was given to her. The arguments became intensely hurtful. Carlos and Maria quarreled about anything and everything, and soon, for the first time in their years of marriage, Maria considered leaving her husband.

The tension between them soon began to ease, however, as Carlos found another focus for his anger. He had never liked Marcus, the friend who was driving the car the night Juan was killed, and Marcus had been drinking and driving too fast at the time of the accident. Initially, Carlos and Maria felt some sympathy for their son's friend because he had been injured seriously and might not ever walk again. But after many miserable months, when Carlos's anger at himself and Maria had brought him no consolation, all remaining sympathy for the boy abruptly ended.

The more Carlos thought about it, the more Marcus became the primary object of Carlos's wrath. One Sunday morning after worship, Carlos saw Marcus in a wheelchair pushed by his parents. In a voice loud enough for everyone leaving the church to hear, Carlos shouted curses and accusations. Marcus's father stepped between the two and challenged Carlos. Several members of the congregation quickly intervened to avoid a fight.

For weeks, Carlos's thoughts were obsessed with wishing harm to Marcus. When Marcus's DWI charges finally came to court, Carlos was there. He wanted the court to put Marcus in prison for Juan's death. The judge allowed Carlos to speak, but his words had no effect on the outcome. Marcus's lawyer already had worked out a plea bargain with the county prosecutor. The eighteen-year-old was convicted of DWI and reckless driving. His license was suspended for a year, and he had to pay a fine.

Carlos now became furious at the justice system. He began to refer to it as the *injustice* system. Every representative of government authority suddenly became Carlos's enemy. Once, when he was stopped by a police officer for a traffic violation, instead of attempting to talk his way out of the ticket, Carlos verbally exploded.

Carlos no longer raged at Maria, but things were not the same between them. That remained true even after their financial windfall. A personal injury lawyer had approached Carlos and Maria shortly after the accident, and eventually the insurance company covering Marcus's car settled for just over a million dollars. Even after the attorney received his cut, there remained enough to pay off all their debts, buy a new car, and buy a house in a more affluent neighborhood. But despite his improved surroundings, Carlos remained angry.

Months turned into years. Carlos now aimed his anger consciously at God. He stopped going to church and began to question everything he ever had been taught about God. "How can God be good if God lets such bad things happen?" he asked. "If God is able to perform miracles, why didn't God perform one that night?" Carlos now believed God was the one who ultimately and truly was to blame for Juan's death, and he was determined to live his own life as a protest against God's cruelty.

One day, at the secret request of Maria, their minister came by to visit. Carlos liked Pastor Rick, but he was not pleased to see him. "You are wasting your time, Pastor," Carlos said. "I refuse to believe in a God who allows such terrible things to happen. Don't waste your time on me. I am so mad at God that I am sure God does not want anything to do with me. Go away, Pastor. There is nothing you can say that will make any difference."

"So you are angry with God," Pastor Rick said softly. "Do you think you are the first person ever to be angry with God? Do you think you are the only one who ever questioned God? Let me assure you, Carlos, God can handle our anger just fine. But I am concerned about you. I am worried about what it is doing to Carlos. You appear to have gotten yourself stuck in your anger. That is not a good thing for you, Carlos, or for Maria, or for anyone else close to you."

A week later the minister was back, and Maria made them another pot of coffee.

"Last time we spoke," Pastor Rick began, "you said you didn't care about what your anger is doing to you. I truly would like to know whether you care about *anything* right now. What *do* you care about, Carlos? You are not the only hurt soul in this world. There are others hurting all around you. Have you considered how much pain Maria is in? She also lost a son. Have you thought for one moment how you have multiplied that pain because you are so angry? And have you considered that our church is filled with people who are suffering? Maybe not over the death of a son, but with suffering that is also real."

A flush of fresh anger came over Carlos. "I know there is suffering in the world! That is what makes me so angry with God! Why did God make a world in which all this suffering happens? And don't say it's because of sin. Because I know there are a lot of terrible sinners out there doing just fine and a lot of good people in this world who have had very bad things happen to them."

"You are right," the pastor responded. "Our Lord once was asked whether some men who were killed when a tower fell on them were worse sinners than others. The Lord told his questioners that those men had not sinned any more than anyone else.[17]

"That is the way life is, Carlos," the pastor continued. "Bad things happen. Make no mistake. Sometimes it *is* because of our sin. And sometimes it is because of the sin of others. But sometimes tragedies just *happen*. As we learned as children from the Humpty Dumpty nursery rhyme, sometimes there is a great fall, and things are so broken they can never be put back together again. But it is not always because somebody pushed. Sometimes there is nobody to blame. Does God allow these bad things to happen? You bet. Do I understand why? Not really. A lot of people try to explain these things, but the truth is that we human beings are incapable of understanding the ways of God."

Carlos stared into his half-empty cup.

"Carlos," the pastor continued, "we may not be able to understand the reason why bad things happen to us, but we *are* capable of understanding that God wants us to do something besides feel sorry for ourselves or wallow in our anger. I am going to ask you what I believe God is asking you: Have you learned anything from your loss? Have you allowed yourself to grow spiritually through your suffering? You say you can't help being angry. But have you called upon God to help you heal? Have you asked God to take away your anger? Have you opened your heart and let God comfort you?

"You say you are upset about all the tragedy in the world. If you are so concerned, what are you doing about it? Do you really care, or are you too busy enjoying your resentment? Are you going to continue to indulge your resentment until it destroys your soul?"

During the days that followed, Carlos attempted to dismiss the pastor's words and not think about them. But he could not get them out of his mind. One Friday night, unable to focus on anything else, he tossed and turned sleeplessly, well into the early morning hours. Sometime before dawn, being careful not to disturb Maria, he slipped out of bed, and went to a guest room where he knelt beside the bed. For the first time in a very long time, he prayed.

He asked God to forgive him. He asked Juan to forgive him. He vowed he would ask Maria in the morning to forgive him. He prayed for the willingness to forgive Juan's friend, Marcus. He prayed for guidance and for God to help him move beyond his anger so he might be able again to feel the pain of others and help them. He prayed, through tears, for a long time. He finally went to bed as dawn was breaking. He fell asleep without effort and slept most of the day. It was his best sleep in a very long time.

On Sunday, Carlos surprised Maria by attending church with her. He was still feeling estranged from God, but then something happened to him that helped him feel less so.

The reality that had angered Carlos more than anything during the years since Juan's death was that his son had died so young. Carlos was haunted by the consciousness of all that Juan might have experienced and accomplished in the years that were snatched from him. Each time he thought about it, he was filled with resentment.

But as Carlos sat in church that day, his eyes were drawn to a stained glass window containing a picture of Jesus dying on the cross. He realized, perhaps consciously for the first time, that Jesus had died a very young man. It occurred to Carlos that God knew better than anyone how he felt. In the midst of that insight, Carlos was aware of a warming in the region of his heart. A voice within him seemed to be saying, "God knows and God cares." It was a moment of healing. Carlos tried to conceal his tears from those around him.

A few Sundays later, he listened attentively to Pastor Rick's sermon. The topic of the day was anger. As Carlos listened, he suspected that Pastor Rick had prepared this sermon with a particular parishioner in mind.

"When our anger is aimed at God," Pastor Rick said, "we believe we will find resolution for our pain in the rightness of our position. We believe our anger is justified because we have experienced what we believe to be the injustice of God. Now, it is difficult to war with God. As Job recognized, there is no way to win a direct challenge to the Almighty. So when we are angry with God, we usually take an indirect approach. We may protest, as Job did, by asking God to end our lives, to finish the job, so to speak. And sometimes we displace that anger on some other person or group of persons."[18]

Carlos listened closely. It had taken many years, but he believed God had brought him to this time and place in order to hear this very message.

"One reason we get stuck in our anger," the pastor continued, "is that we have been deluded by our own attempts to justify our resentments. In order to experience healing, it is necessary for us to let go of our justifications. That, of course, is easier said than done. But this is where genuine repentance comes in. As Christians, we turn to God in prayer. We pray for forgiveness and for the grace to forgive ourselves and others. We pray for those toward whom our anger has been directed. We pray to be restored to a loving relationship with God and with all our neighbors. We pray that our grief will be healed by the One who desires to heal us, who is able to change our suffering into loving care toward others."

Carlos took these words to heart. In time, Carlos underwent a transformation, and with it came a change in his attitude toward Maria, toward Marcus, and toward God. He felt a new peace, and he was able to know freedom from the terrible bitterness that had eaten away at his soul for so long.

## Your Story

1. Read Genesis 4:3–6. Why do you think people feel angry when life does not go the way they planned? Whom do you tend to blame when it happens to you?

2. Have you ever known someone who was stuck in anger toward God? How did that person act out his or her anger?

3. Read Proverbs 29:22 and Matthew 5:21–22. Why is anger a dangerous emotion for Christians?

4. Give examples of the ways in which people try to justify their anger. Why is it so hard to let go of our resentments?

5. Read 1 Corinthians 10:13. How does God help people of faith overcome their anger and resentments?

8

# DEPRESSION
## Never Put a Period Where a Comma Belongs

*We are hard pressed on every side, but not crushed; perplexed,*
*but not in despair; persecuted, but not abandoned; struck*
*down, but not destroyed.*

2 CORINTHIANS 4:8–9

When we think about a person in grief, we tend to picture someone sorrowful with a downcast demeanor. We may recall a particular friend or acquaintance whose eyes sometimes filled with tears at unexpected moments and who occasionally wept convulsively.

However, many faces of grief do not fit this stereotype. A person in denial, running away, feeling like a victim, questioning, or expressing anger may not appear to be grieving. But those expressions of emotional pain are as valid in their own periods of grief as the emotions of sadness and depression are in theirs.

The stereotype of grief as depression fails to portray the diversity of the grieving process. Nevertheless, deep sadness is the most common of all the periods of grieving, and also the most painful.

## Tears

In our culture, crying tends to be associated with infants and with weakness. We have been conditioned to believe it is wrong for adults to cry. Both men and women are likely to feel this way at times, but it is especially true for males. Simply put, tears are thought not to be manly. So when we have tearful moments or episodes of uncontrollable sobbing after a loss, we can feel foolish, embarrassed, and out of control. And when this happens, we become more depressed because we feel that we are losing courage. Afterward, we may try even harder to hold back the tears, and in doing so we deny ourselves the kind of emotional release that can help us heal.

We need to understand that tearful episodes in the midst of our sorrows are natural and healthy. When a loved one has died, such moments may be occasioned by memory-evoking events such as anniversaries, birthdays, or holidays, by places where special moments once were shared, and by objects associated with the deceased, such as a pair of glasses or strands of hair in a comb. It is normal to have such tearful moments even many years after a loss. At such times, we reexperience the pain and loneliness of our earlier grieving.

Grieving tears, we are told by scientists, are chemically different from other tears. When we are in emotional pain, our bodies produce chemicals and hormones that dramatically lower our mood. Crying releases pain relievers and mood elevators into the bloodstream. Tears chemically soothe our sadness. That is the physiological reason we feel better after crying.

There is also a psychological and spiritual effect. Crying releases the internal pressure of emotional pain. We cry to release our suffering and to cleanse our inner visions. Through tears, we symbolically wash away our pain. Such baths may be needed frequently for a period of time and maybe for the rest of our lives.

It is interesting to contrast our current Western cultural attitude toward tears with that of biblical peoples. In ancient Israel, men and women wept openly during times of intense feeling. The stories of Jacob and Esau and of Joseph and his brothers tell of weeping during emotionally charged moments of reconciliation, and tears are associated with grief throughout the Scriptures. We read of David crying over the death of his son Absalom, of Jeremiah's fountain of tears over the fall of

Jerusalem, of Jesus weeping over the sins of that same city, of the bitter tears of Simon Peter after he had denied Jesus three times, and of Mary weeping at Jesus' tomb, to mention only a few relevant passages.[19]

That tears are associated with all kinds of human suffering in the Bible is underscored by the promises of hope we find there.

Weeping may remain for a night, but rejoicing comes in the morning. (Ps. 30:5)

Those who sow in tears will reap with songs of joy. (Ps. 126:5)

He will wipe every tear from their eyes. There will be no more death or mourning or crying or pain, for the old order of things has passed away. (Rev. 21:4)

**Depression and Healing**

Not only can tears have a salving effect, but depression itself can have healing benefits. When we are physically sick, our bodies warn us that we need to rest and take care of ourselves for a while until we begin to recover. When we are very ill, we often find we are unable to continue with all but the most basic activities of daily living, and sometimes we need the assistance of others even for those. When we show signs of feeling better, an indication that we are beginning the process of recovery, we need to begin resuming normal activities. If we remain in the sick role, we will lose ground physically and might eventually lose the capacity to get better.

Feelings of depression are comparable to the way we experience ourselves when we are physically sick. In addition to physical stamina, the challenges of daily living require emotional and spiritual energy. When we are depressed, we may not feel like getting out of bed in the morning, bathing, grooming, getting dressed, or going out. This inclination toward personal neglect is likely to be accompanied by an absence of motivation to do even the simplest of household duties.

When we are in deep sorrow, we also may experience intense loneliness that feels like abandonment. This can be true even when our grief is not about the loss of a loved one. Our feelings of aloneness arise in part from the sense that nobody knows what we are going through. We believe that others are unable to understand, and we think that if they really did know how we feel, they might not love us or approve of our struggle.

As bad as all of this may seem, depression can be a necessary stage on our journey toward recovery. Just as the tiredness and weakness we feel when we are physically ill can play a positive role in bodily healing, emotional depression serves a similar function in our lives when we have been traumatized by a loss. Melancholy can force us to slow down, to reduce our activities, to increase our rest, and to distinguish between what is important and unimportant in our lives.

## Dangerous Depression

As with other stages of grief, we need to remember that any potential benefit from a depressed mood is short-lived. Just as the prolonging of the sick role can lead to further loss of health, so the extension of a season of sadness beyond its appointed time has the potential to do great harm.

While it is normal and sometimes necessary for us to be depressed during grief, in some people a tragic loss can trigger a serious episode of an underlying depressive illness. People with feelings of worthlessness, hopelessness, excessive guilt, and thoughts of suicide may be suffering biochemically from a psychiatric disorder. If such symptoms are present, we must consult a physician, because clinical depression generally requires medication and counseling in order to address the underlying conditions. When medically appropriate, medication should not be seen as an alternative to the grieving journey but as an important tool for surviving the darkest days of grief.

Our concern here, however, is not so much the need some of us may have for medical attention but the need all of us may have for spiritual guidance. Many of us who become stuck in depression do so not because of an underlying psychiatric condition but because we are having difficulty continuing our journey toward accepting the reality of our losses. *While depression can move us toward healing, it also may bring the spiritual temptation to give up on life.* To take overt action on suicidal thoughts is usually an indication of clinical depression. But other forms of giving up can tempt us during the sadness of our grief. This *hidden suicide* may be expressed as the long-term decision not to feel, not to put forth effort, not to do anything but muddle through each day.

Once we decide life is not worth living, we may decide to give in to depression, to let others take care of us, to yield to a life without the possibility of hope or joy. Or we may take an opposite approach and instead of shutting down, we adopt a high-risk lifestyle. This sometimes takes the form of pursuing daily oblivion through immoral behaviors and mind-altering substances without regard to consequences. This hopelessness, this giving up, may be an indication of clinical depression, but when there is no underlying mental disease, it is more likely to be a case of spiritual despair.

*Depression is hazardous because every day that we stay in its grip, we have more difficulty rising above it.* Depression can become a downward spiral. When our mood remains low for very long, we are in danger of falling into despair and becoming stuck in perpetual sadness.

About two years after the onset of my son's mental illness, I fell into a deep depression. The burden and constant stress of trying to care for him and manage his behavior with no promise of relief or recovery in sight was more than I could bear. Over a period of several months, I felt myself slipping deeper and deeper into despair. It was a frightening feeling, something like being on a plane in a steep dive and about to crash. I had been expending every bit of spiritual energy I could find taking care of my son. My cup was empty. One day I decided that I needed to make some kind of major change in order to take care of myself, or I would have nothing left for him.

For many years, I had thought about returning to school in order to work on a doctorate. I decided to investigate my options, and several months later I was accepted into a graduate program at the University of North Carolina. I do not necessarily recommend graduate school to everyone as an effective treatment for depression! But it was just what I needed. My son's condition had not changed, but my life no longer felt swallowed up by overwhelming tragedy. By structuring my days so that some time was devoted to my personal goals, I gained a new sense of purpose and direction for myself. I had reason to hope again. I am convinced God was at work in my decision. My new studies helped prepare me for what would soon become a new calling.

Sometimes we are fortunate enough to be able make new choices about our lives that reverse the downward spiral of depression. But just as it may be impossible to climb out of clinical depression without medical assistance, so it is not always possible to escape the pit of spiritual despair on our own. *When we are stuck in depression, feeling powerless in the face of it, we need to remember that there is one thing we are always able to do: we can ask for help.* To do so is not an indication of weakness but a sign of strength. It is a faith response. Not to do so can be a deadly form of unfaith.

## Depression and the Spiritual Journey

Depression may be dangerous, but it also can serve as a catalyst for spiritual growth. In order to grow spiritually, we need to feel our emotional pain. We need to be able to identify with the suffering of others. Depression can make that happen and serve to detach us from everyday concerns and awaken us to our spiritual essence. The spiritual function of grief is to cleanse the soul of bitter feelings, not to multiply them. That is why it is important during times of depression not to neglect the practices of our faith.

When we fall into despair, the help we need might come to us through the Scriptures, through a sermon, during a time of prayer, or in some other moment when we have opened our inner selves to God's healing. Or it might come from a spiritual counselor or a person of faith who is a good friend—one reason we need to maintain our friendships even when we do not feel like doing so. In any case, we need to hold on to the promises of our faith. We need to hold on to hope and not let go. We need to ask God for help and trust that help will come in God's time. And we need to get out into the world and start engaging with life again. As long as we have the gift of life, there is life to be lived and a journey to be completed.

**Angela's Story**

For the fourth time in a little more than three years, nineteen-year-old Angela was involuntarily committed to a psychiatric facility. Once again she had attempted suicide.

The first time Angela had shown signs of suicidal behavior was a few weeks before her sixteenth birthday. That attempt was little more than a dangerous gesture in which she made small cuts on her wrists, too superficial to do any damage. The next three tries, however, took the form of serious pill overdoses, combinations of over-the-counter pain relievers and the medications psychiatrists had prescribed for her depression.

Each of Angela's hospitalizations ranged from two to four weeks. In the months between hospitalizations, Angela spent much of her time engaging in behaviors designed to kill her emotional pain. She drank a lot and often drove while intoxicated. She smoked a considerable amount of marijuana and spent long hours in a stoned stupor. She engaged in casual sex with men she met in clubs and bars, so many times she had lost count. But her pain persisted.

Angela's behavior was a far cry from her earlier teen years. She had been an active participant and leader in her church youth group. She had taken several mission trips to Appalachia and to hurricane-damaged areas to help people repair and build back their homes. She had attended spiritual retreats and Christian concerts with her group. She was respected for her sincere faith and exemplary behavior. At school she was regarded as someone who was a little too well-behaved but likable nevertheless.

Then Angela met Tony. She was fifteen, and Tony, a freshman at a local university, had just turned eighteen. Tony was strikingly handsome and fun loving, and he owned a car. Angela was immediately smitten. Both of them constantly thought about the other, their first experience with this kind of love.

Because Angela was only fifteen, her parents were not happy about the relationship. Her father was particularly upset about it, but her mother insisted that Angela was mature for her age and that Tony was a nice young man. She was concerned that it might be a serious mistake to forbid their daughter to see him. Instead, they demanded considerable accountability for the time the two were together. They were not allowed to go out together often, and when they did, Angela's parents insisted on knowing where the couple planned to go, who would be there, what they would be doing, and when Angela would be home.

When Tony and Angela had been dating for about three months, her father came home unexpectedly to find the two of them having sex in Angela's bedroom. Exploding with anger, he called the police. That call was like hurling a stone—once thrown, it could never be retrieved. Tony was arrested. Because of the age difference and the laws in their state concerning sex with a minor, he was charged with sexual assault and held in jail. The arresting officers treated him roughly, he was fingerprinted, and one of the officers informed him that if convicted, he could be sentenced to twenty years and would be listed permanently on the sex-offender registry. Alone in jail late that night, Tony tore up his shirt and made it into a makeshift rope. He hanged himself from the metal screen that covered the overhead light in his cell.

The night after she watched Tony's casket descend into the ground, Angela cut her wrists. When she emerged from the bathroom bleeding, her parents rushed her to the hospital.

Now, more than three years later, the psychiatrist assigned to Angela was a young female resident. In conversations over several days, she laid the groundwork for a therapeutic relationship. One day, fully anticipating Angela's answer, the psychiatrist asked, "What is the worst thing that ever happened to you?"

Angela's eyes filled with tears as she remembered Tony and recounted the circumstances of his death.

"How do you feel about Tony now?"

"I still love him and miss him."

"Is that all?"

"I feel like if it wasn't for me, he would still be alive. And I am really mad at my dad for calling the police on him."

"What else do you feel?"

After a long pause, Angela said, "I am really angry Tony did what he did. I know he was really upset about things, but he didn't have to kill himself."

"I want you to write a letter to Tony," the doctor said. "I want you to tell him how you feel about what he did. Can you do that?"

Angela sat down that night to write her letter. She started slowly. But soon the words burst forth from some long-locked chamber within her. She told Tony how much she loved and missed him. She told him how sorry she was for placing him in danger, and how responsible she felt because her father called the police. But then, with tears dripping on the page and smudging some of the words, she told Tony that what he had done was stupid and selfish. She told him she knew he had been in a lot of trouble and felt a lot of fear and emotional pain, but she also knew that if he had not killed himself, he somehow could have gotten through it. Other people had gotten through worse things. Why, she wanted to know, could he not see that his life was not over?

The next day she handed several limp pages to her therapist, who read them slowly and then said, "I see someone put a period where there should have been a comma."

Angela looked embarrassed and puzzled. "I was never very good in English."

"Oh, I'm not talking about your punctuation. I'm talking about what you said to Tony. That is what you said, isn't it? Tony put a period in his life where a comma belonged."

"I ... I guess so."

The therapist leaned forward, looked her patient in the eye, and spoke gently but firmly. "How about you, Angela? Have you put a period in your life where a comma belongs? I am not just talking about your attempts to kill yourself, though you have attempted to do exactly what Tony did, four different times. You also have put a pretty effective period on your own life through your partying, your boozing, your drugging, and your sexual activity."

Angela nodded.

"You started all of this when you were fifteen," the therapist continued. "Because of the way you have chosen to handle your grief, you now are a nineteen-year-old stuck at the emotional maturity level of a fifteen-year-old. In fact, I take that back. You have regressed to the emotional state of a child who refuses to recognize that life has legitimate limits, and in the process you have missed three good years of your life that you will never have back. Yes, what happened to you was a terrible thing. But you could have gotten through it if *you* had not decided your life was over."

Angela began to sob uncontrollably, and the therapist spent the rest of their session holding and comforting her patient.

That became a turning point in Angela's life. As she lay awake that night, she remembered how life had been for her before she started dating Tony. She remembered how she used to believe in God and that God had a purpose for her life. As she drifted off to sleep, she prayed for the first time in a very long time. She prayed that God would help her find her purpose.

The next day, Angela asked to see the hospital chaplain. The chaplain was a man in his forties with kind eyes and a gentle voice. Angela had seen him on the wards during previous hospitalizations, but this was the first time she had spoken with him. She filled him in on her story and then said, "I have made such a mess of my life, I don't know what to do now. I don't want to do what Tony did. I don't want to stop living, but I don't know how to start again. What do I need to do?"

"Unlike your boyfriend's self-destruction, or the way it would have been had you succeeded in taking your own life, you still have a life and you still have a future," the chaplain counseled. "You speak of your old love as if he were the only one who ever cared for you. I am betting you have people now who love you, who care for you, and who are hurting because you are hurting."

"I know I've hurt my mom and dad. I wish I could undo all the ways I've let them down."

"We can't change the past, Angela. But we can change our relationship to the present. We can change the future, and we can reach out to others for help."

"I just wish I could turn the clock back to that awful day and change what happened," Angela said.

"Have you ever heard of Marilyn Monroe?" the chaplain asked.

"I think so. Wasn't she that blonde actress who died of a drug overdose a long time ago?"

"That's right. Did you know that Marilyn Monroe had a terrible childhood? She was sexually abused. She had a terrible mother. Later, as a famous actress, she became engaged to a well-known playwright named Arthur Miller. She was very excited and happy at the time. As she was preparing for the wedding, some members of the press interviewed her. One of them, knowing about her troubled past, asked her, 'Miss Monroe, if you could, would you change anything about your life up to this point?'"

Angela waited expectantly for the answer.

"The actress hesitated just a moment before she said, 'Of course there are many things in my past I wish had not happened. I wouldn't want them to happen to anyone. But if by going back and changing one thing it would mean I would not be here today, preparing for this wedding, I wouldn't change a thing.' At that moment, Marilyn Monroe voiced a very important truth. Unfortunately, she later forgot about her own amazing insight."

"You mean because she overdosed on drugs," Angela concluded.

"Have you ever done something you wish you could go back and undo?"

"There are times when we all wish we could go back and change some things in our past. I can think of several occasions when I would have liked to start over and make different decisions. Some of those had to do with major turning points in my life. But if I could go back and change something, my whole life would be different than it has been. I wouldn't be the chaplain at this hospital, and I wouldn't be sitting here with you right now. And Angela, I know in my heart today that I am exactly where I am supposed to be."

"I know I'm glad you are here, you and my psychiatrist."

"Don't ever waste your energies trying to change the past, Angela. There is a story in the Bible about the wife of a man named Lot who looked back at a disaster behind her. She turned into a pillar of salt.[20] If we get hung up on the terrible things in our past, we can't change and move forward. We become like pillars of salt."

"You mean sort of paralyzed. Is that what you think has been happening to me?

"What do you think, Angela? A lot of young people do every day what you and your boyfriend did, with very different results. It was not possible for you to have seen at the time what the outcome was going to be. But no matter how unwise or wrong our acts, no matter how tragic the result of our actions, the past is the past. You need to focus on living now, on making the decisions that are needed now to turn your life around. And here is the miraculous truth about what God can do: God can take our crummy pasts that we can't change and use them for good if we will let him."

"I would like to believe that. But it's hard to imagine right now."

"What we are talking about, Angela," the chaplain continued, "is one of the most important themes of the Bible. The Bible mostly is about people who messed up. Some of them messed up again and again. But God kept giving them new chances to turn things around. Even when the results of their messing up were really bad, God found a way to give them another chance. It also tells us about people who had terrible things happen to them that were not their fault. Some things didn't happen because the people messed up. They just happened. Stuff happens in life. But God also was able to turn those things into good. Don't ask me how God does this. I can't understand it. But I have experienced it, and I have witnessed it many times. And that is what the Bible promises.[21]

"Angela, you can experience it too. It will not be easy. But if you ask, God will help you."

Angela's story might have ended differently, as it does in so many lives when suicide is considered. She could have been back in the hospital a few months later, or her grieving parents could have watched her coffin being lowered into the ground, as Angela had watched Tony's. But that is not how Angela's story turned out. Angela never again attempted suicide and never again returned to a psychiatric hospital. And she did discover what she believed was God's purpose for her life as she experienced the psalmist's words: "Though I walk in the midst of trouble, you preserve my life" (Ps. 138:7).

## *Your Story*

1. Read Jeremiah 9:1 and Psalm 30:5. When is the last time you shed tears? Why are tears important to the healing process?

2. Sometimes the decisions people make have irreversible negative consequences. What are some decisions you have made that illustrate this point?

3. Can you think of persons who succeeded in putting periods in their lives where commas belonged? Was their "suicide" direct or indirect?

4. If you could change one thing in your past, what would it be? What is the lesson of the Marilyn Monroe story that the chaplain told Angela?

5. Read 2 Corinthians 4:8–9. What do you think you can do in the present to minimize the possibility that you will be tempted in the future to put a period in your life where a comma belongs?

## STEP 4

# RECOGNIZE MOMENTS OF GRACE

If we have spiritual eyes to see, the journey of grief is filled with moments of grace, revealing God's loving presence comforting and guiding us toward healing.

*Blessed are your eyes because they see,*
*and your ears because they hear.*
MATTHEW 13:16

*I will turn their mourning into gladness;*
*I will give them comfort and joy instead of sorrow.*
JEREMIAH 31:13

*The LORD has done great things for us,*
*and we are filled with joy.*
PSALM 126:3

*Though outwardly we are wasting away, yet inwardly*
*we are being renewed day by day.*
2 CORINTHIANS 4:16

# 9

# ACCEPTANCE

## The Road to Recovery Is Paved with Moments of Grace

*Not only so, but we also rejoice in our sufferings, because we
know that suffering produces perseverance; perseverance,
character; and character, hope. And hope does not disappoint
us, because God has poured out his love into our hearts by the
Holy Spirit, whom he has given us.*

ROMANS 5:3–5

As suggested throughout previous chapters, grief is a normal response to a significant loss. The journey of grief can be a pathway
to healing, but whether healing takes place depends a great deal on
the choices we make along the way. The grief journey is not a comfortable ride on an aircraft in which we have no responsibility until
it is time to disembark. It is more like a marathon over treacherous
terrain, requiring personal commitment, great effort, willingness to
experience pain, strategy, pacing, endurance, and determination to
reach the goal.

Unlike marathon runners, however, we do not have to rely entirely
upon ourselves in order to complete this pilgrimage. The rules of the
journey of grief allow and encourage us to ask for and receive assistance.
*Failing to ask for help probably is the single greatest reason people get bogged
down along the way.* Professionals, friends, and loved ones desire to assist
us, if only we are willing to ask. And above all, if we have eyes of faith,

we can see that God continually is reaching out to help us and guide us through our dark valleys to a place of healing.

It has been said that time heals all things—but that just is not so. Many people get stuck in one or more stages of grief and never reach acceptance. For people of faith, a more accurate way to understand how healing comes about is this: *God will heal us in his time if we are willing to live in reality and walk in faith.* Our responsibility on the journey of grief is to find that willingness so that we might, with God's help, experience the grace to embrace the changed reality of our lives.

## The Gift of Acceptance

The seasons of grief are times for emotional and spiritual work. But acceptance does not come about through our efforts alone. It is a gift of grace, whether or not we acknowledge it as such. During our time of grief, God is working on our behalf every step of the way. Acceptance is the goal of our journey, but *we* do not find *it*. It finds us when, in God's time, we are ready for it.

We know we have reached acceptance when we are no longer in denial, no longer trying to run away, no longer playing the victim role. Acceptance also means we have stopped questioning God's goodness and have begun trusting God's love for us. And acceptance is the end of blaming, a halt to feelings of despair, and the absence of the impulse to give up.

There is a life-and-death difference between a journey of grief that ends in depression and one that leads to acceptance. Depression is resignation without tranquility, without the willingness to adapt, without hope, and without confidence in God. Acceptance is surrender with serenity accompanied by the willingness to change. And acceptance is hope-filled anticipation with trust in God's comfort and care.

## The Willingness to Let Go

In order for acceptance to be real, it must be a letting go of the past and of the persons, things, or circumstances we have lost. If we fail to let go, we are at risk of becoming the psychological equivalent of Lot's wife.[22] We are in danger of becoming emotionally frozen, and over time we may lose our ability to cope with the present and engage the future. *While acceptance involves releasing, it does not mean forgetting.* If we forget, we cannot learn life's lessons. A divorce, for example, contains lessons about life that inform the present and the future. And a marriage usually is a storehouse of memories that have shaped both spouses and could be important to children, relatives, and friends. If that is the case, then letting go should not mean the destruction of those memories. Rather, what is called for is the grateful acknowledgement of the blessings of the past, free of imprisonment to what is no more.

We disrespect the past when we remain burdened with regrets or continue to obsess over its passing. When we know acceptance, we no longer feel that we must rewrite the past. We trust that God can and will mysteriously bring good out of what has been. And we are free to get on with the task of living, creating the story of our future.

Similarly, when our loved ones have died, we do not reach acceptance until we are willing to let go. But letting go does not mean we are supposed to forget those who have been dear to us. The wonderful moments we shared with them are treasures that never can be taken away from us. Nor does releasing the past mean the end of our love. If we truly love another, that love does not end with death. It is important to find a place in our hearts where those who have shared our journey can remain and where they always will be loved and honored.

It is also helpful to honor and remember our loved ones in ways that symbolize who they were, what their lives meant to others, and how much we continue to love them. The desire to *memorialize* is a deeply felt human need, often accompanied by spontaneous acts. All of us are familiar with roadside memorials that spring up where people have been killed in accidents. When we devote aesthetic objects, significant places, special times, and simple rituals to remember the unique and unrepeatable lives of our loved ones, we are trying to find healing. Long after funerals and memorial services, such symbols can continue to provide healthy ways to honor those who have died even as we are learning to let go.

If we forget the past, we fail to respect it. But if we cling too much to what has been, we may be in danger of dishonoring it even more. It is important to remember that those who genuinely have loved us would not want us to condemn ourselves to a lifetime of sorrow. When a personal tragedy happens, we may feel for a time that it would be wrong to experience happiness ever again. Acceptance means we have reached the point on our journey where we again can feel the joy God desires to bestow upon us. Happiness is not a failure to honor the past. In a profound way, it honors those who are no longer with us and their unending wishes for us to be happy, to know true joy.

## The Willingness to Change

But acceptance is more than the willingness to release the past. It also is about the willingness to change. A life-changing loss brings with it the need for *practical* alterations. These alterations require realistic actions. In the early stages of grief, it is usually best for us to make only minor changes in our daily lives. Familiar routines and our networks of family and friends can bring us great comfort and should be disturbed as little as possible. For this reason, many grief counselors recommend waiting a year after a loss before making any major change, such as a long-distance move.

Over time, however, the practical changes we need to make usually become clear to us. The nature of these, of course, depends upon individual circumstances and on the kinds of personal tragedies experienced. Those who lose the use of a limb in an accident or in combat, for example, may need to make changes in their living environments and develop new skills for managing the activities of daily living. Parents of teenage children who have had an onset of mental illness may need to alter their work schedules in order to provide twenty-four-hour-a-day monitoring. A young stay-at-home wife may need to find a job after her husband has betrayed and abandoned her. And a widow may need to move closer to relatives or find a roommate.

While these are only examples of possibilities, they illustrate the truth that when it comes to change, one size does *not* fit all. One clear indication that we have reached at least a degree of acceptance is our willingness to identify the specific, practical changes necessary for our particular journeys. And of course, acceptance means that this recognition is followed by the development of realistic plans, followed in turn by necessary actions.

But practical matters are not the only things requiring change. *Every personal tragedy is an opportunity to grow spiritually.* The apostle Paul found suffering capable of producing perseverance, then character, then hope. Acceptance means we are willing for God to help us mature in our faith.

To live in acceptance means we are open to learning even the most difficult lessons from our experiences. The time of acceptance is a time for letting go of old attitudes and the cultivation of new ones. Our sufferings can help us develop a better understanding of life and the mystery of God's care for us, and they can lead us to a greater awareness of the suffering of others, thereby opening avenues of service to God and neighbor.

### God's Comfort and Care

*Acceptance also is characterized by the desire to be healed and the willingness to trust the Healer.* The healings of Jesus recorded in the Gospels underscore the importance of the petitioner's faith. In order for healing to occur, typically it was necessary for people to want and ask for healing. They also had to trust that Jesus could and would heal them.

Our healing may not come to us as suddenly as those in the Bible. Physical healing sometimes takes a long time. So does spiritual healing. But whether recovery from our grieving occurs quickly or over an extended period, the desire to be healed and the willingness to trust in God's comfort and care remain prerequisites.

The grace of God that comforts, sustains, and transforms us as people of faith comes to us when we open our hearts to receive it. We may find ourselves finally ready to accept this grace only when we have hit bottom, feel defeated, have nowhere else to turn, and cry out to God for help. But willingness also may come to us in less dramatic moments, especially when we as people of faith are in the midst of praying, reading and studying the Scriptures, attending worship, or participating in the sacred rituals of our various traditions. These are tried and true activities that help us open ourselves to God. It is no accident that these activities are sometimes called *means of grace.*

God also works grace in us in other mysterious ways. Sometimes it happens in a moment of sudden illumination, when a thought presses upon us that we immediately know comes from God. Sometimes it happens when we are struck by a demonstration of the majesty and beauty of God's creation and feel a warm peace wash over us. At other times it happens because we encounter another human being whose presence, words, and actions become the channel through which God speaks to us. Such times are *moments of grace,* and through them God works healing in us.

When we are on the journey of grief, it is important to pay attention, to notice, and to listen for God to speak, comfort, and guide. For people of faith, there are no coincidences in life. God is at work in all things.

## David's Story

When Rachel arrived home from the doctor that day, having been given the diagnosis of cancer and a prognosis of a year to live, her husband, David, saw the evidence of shock, fear, and sorrow on her face. He tried to comfort and assure her as best he could, but it was difficult to transcend his own feeling that he could not possibly deal with this.

Those who knew Rachel thought of her as wonderful, even irreplaceable in their lives. The nursing staff at the hospital appreciated her for her kind and wise management style. Her personal friends experienced her as a compassionate spiritual presence. David knew both sets of extended family loved Rachel and would be devastated by her passing. Yet he knew that all of these people would be able to grieve for a while and then get their lives back to normal.

But Rachel was *his* soul mate, the love of his *life*. How could he watch her suffer and die? How could he survive such a great loss? How could life ever be normal for him again? And how could he possibly stand to experience the pain of his three children as they lost the mother who had nurtured them, whom they adored and depended on? It was all too horrible to contemplate.

It was not long before David discovered that the reality of Rachel's battle would be much worse than he had imagined. She grew weaker and more dependent on him each day, requiring him to take an extended leave from work to assist with her care. A hospice nurse began making daily visits. The last two weeks were especially difficult. Rachel had no appetite; her body was starving. David watched as she drifted into a coma; he grimaced in the middle of the night when she moaned in pain. Physically and emotionally burned out, he pleaded tearfully with God to free Rachel from her misery. Yet despite his daily trauma and perpetual exhaustion, he was able to get through till the end because Rachel had shown him how.

Three years after Rachel's death, David walked to the podium as the speaker at a large interfaith breakfast. Because of the recommendation of his own pastor, David had been invited to talk about how faith had sustained and assisted him through his personal tragedy. As he reflected on the experience of Rachel's death, he felt completely undeserving of being held up as an example of strong faith in the midst of difficulty. He was painfully aware of the weakness of his personal faith and of those times when he was tempted to abandon his faith altogether along the way. At first he declined the invitation to speak.

Upon reflection, however, it dawned on David that the speech was not about what *he* had done. It was not about *his* personal struggle and triumph but what *God* had done to care for him along the way. David knew that the real story of his life since Rachel had become ill and passed away was that God had given him what he needed, in the midst of his own weakness and personal despair, at each critical stage of dealing with the tragic change in his family. That is why David called back and agreed to be the speaker. And that is why he titled his speech "The Road to Recovery Is Paved with Moments of Grace."

When she was first diagnosed, the doctors had given Rachel a year to live. She survived almost eighteen months. David thought at first it was his job to help Rachel through those difficult times. He found instead that it was *Rachel's* strength and courage that sustained *him* during those terribly difficult months.

David encouraged Rachel to quit work. He told her to take care of herself. While he was away at work and the children were at school, he wanted her to spend more time doing the things she enjoyed. But Rachel chose to keep on working. The hospital was where she felt normal and useful, and working had the added benefit of keeping her health insurance in place so that she would not become a financial burden to her family.

Rachel did arrange to go home most afternoons in time to be with her children. And the family spent many weekends at their second home in the mountains until Rachel became too sick to go there. Her sickness was made greater because she chose an experimental form of chemotherapy in a long-shot effort to find a cure. She knew it probably would not work and would make her physically miserable. But if there was any chance at all that she could beat the odds, it was worth a try. Thinking about her three girls was all the motivation she needed.

Rachel's determination to live her life with courage as a terminally ill person was nothing short of amazing, and David was made stronger by it. "We all are going to die," she would say. "The important thing for any of us is to decide what we are going to do with the time we have left."

Rachel's situation and those words increased David's awareness of his own mortality. He thought more seriously than ever before about what was truly important to him. Rachel's words were a moment of grace for David, a moment when he knew God was speaking to him about his own life.

Perhaps more than by any other events in those final eighteen months with Rachel, David was strengthened by their "happy moments." One night, Rachel and David were about to settle down when Rachel asked him, "What was your happy moment today?"

The question took David completely by surprise. His consciousness had been so saturated by fear and anguish that he found it difficult at first to imagine there had been any happy moments in any recent days.

"My happy moment today," Rachel volunteered, "was when I looked out the kitchen window and saw two hummingbirds drinking from our feeder. What was your happy moment?"

David hesitated. He was not sure he could come up with anything. But then he remembered something. "I guess my happy moment was when I was driving to work this morning. They played one of our songs. It made me remember some of the wonderful times we have shared together." David did not tell Rachel the memories had caused his eyes to fill with tears. But upon reflection, it was, he thought, as close to a happy moment as he could find that day.

After that, Rachel and David agreed to create a nighttime ritual in which each of them would name a happy moment of the day. David was amazed at the way Rachel could be miserable from her treatments and the progression of her disease but still find a happy moment. Sometimes it was in the form of an inspirational e-mail one of her friends had sent her, sometimes a conversation with one of the girls about something at school. Sometimes it was a sunset shared with David or a moment of quiet intimacy with him. Not a day went by that Rachel could not identify her happy moment.

David also was surprised that as the weeks passed, he could identify more easily his own happy moments. He began to anticipate and recognize such moments when they happened, even during the darkest of days. He realized that before Rachel's diagnosis he had missed noticing and appreciating the many little blessings each day held. Now he not only recognized these moments but also understood them as daily gifts from God. When recognized, they provided reassurance that God was with him and with his family in the midst of this terrible thing happening to them. These were significant moments of grace, making strength and endurance possible through the awful times.

David shared all of these things with the more than five hundred people gathered that morning. He also told them about the morning he and Rachel had received the terrible news that the experimental treatments had failed to halt the growth of the tumors. Hospice would need to be called in.

On that gloomy Saturday morning, Rachel and David were drinking coffee silently at the breakfast table when David's father paid them an unexpected visit. A reserved man, never one to demonstrate affection, he had through the years been of a hard-working provider who lived a quiet life of personal integrity. David did not remember a time when his father said he loved him or offered him anything more affectionate than a handshake. But this morning was different.

David's father spoke first to Rachel. He told her how sorry he was that she was going through all of this. He then told both of them about the darkest moment of his own life, when his first daughter, David's younger sister, died just three days after her birth. David knew about his sister's death, but this was the first time he ever had heard his father speak of it.

David's grandfather, who attended the infant's funeral, had the reputation of being even less likely than David's father to express emotion or affection. But David's father now described how at the graveside, as they were burying the baby, David's grandfather placed his arm around his son and told him for the first time that he loved him.

After telling Rachel and David about this important event in his own life, David's father went to each of them in turn. He placed his arms around them and gave each one a big hug and said, "I love you." Then he left. Rachel and David looked at each other in amazement. They were deeply moved. Both of them knew what their happy moment would be for that day.

A week later, David's father, who had survived quadruple bypass a few years earlier, dropped dead of a heart attack. Rachel and David could not help but wonder if the old gentleman somehow had felt a premonition of what was to come the day he uttered those simple but incredibly power-ful words and gave them those memorable hugs.

When he learned of his father's death, David knew he would be bury-ing a father and a wife in the same year. In a strange way, the funeral of his father provided a kind of preparation for Rachel's imminent death. The worship service turned out to be a joyful celebration of his father's life. The pastor reminded those gathered of the promises of God. The children and grandchildren took turns speaking of their love and admi-ration for this quiet, remarkable gentleman.

David knew Rachel's death would be more difficult for him by far than the death of his father. Yet even as he dealt with the trauma and exhaustion of Rachel's last weeks, the shared memories along with the faith and hope of the family for his father's transition to heaven gave him a quiet assurance he had not known before.

When Rachel finally succumbed to her disease, David was over-whelmed with the greatest sense of loss he had ever known. But after watching the love of his life experience pain, grow weak, and fade away during those last few weeks, David also experienced relief. For a while, he felt guilty about his sense of relief because, toward the end, he had prayed for God to take Rachel. But upon reflection, David realized he did not need to feel guilty. He had not prayed for her death for any self-ish reason. His were the prayers of a man who loved his wife and did not want her to suffer.

The memorial service for Rachel packed the church to overflow-ing. Friends and family poured out sympathy and concern. The pas-tor said something that struck home to David: "Feel your grief. Let it happen. And as you permit your sorrow to have its time, remem-ber that 'weeping tarries for the night, but joy comes in the morning light.'" And then the minister recalled a conversation in which Rachel said she had found comfort in a verse from a hymn: "When through the deep waters I cause you to go, the rivers of sorrow will not over-flow."[23]

David had heard these words from Rachel's lips several times over the past eighteen months. He felt certain he could hear Rachel saying them once again through the pastor. They were words meant for him.

A few weeks later, David experienced another important moment of healing. For years prior to her illness, Rachel had enjoyed oil painting. She was accomplished enough to have received a best-in-show award for one of her works in a regional art exhibit. David donated this painting of a large barren oak tree against a sunset background, to the hospital where Rachel worked. The hospital, with donations from staff and friends of Rachel, set aside a small room for prayer and meditation with the picture as a focal point. In a special service conducted by the chaplain, David hung the picture, and the room was dedicated to Rachel's memory.

Rachel had spent considerable time during the final year of her life writing letters and buying presents. She wrote one letter and bought one present for each of her children for each birthday through the age of twenty-one. She attempted to imagine each child at the age of a particular birthday, to buy an age-appropriate gift, and to offer in the letter some good, motherly advice. David was given the responsibility of making sure these gifts and letters were a part of each birthday celebration. After three years and nine such birthdays, David continued to be impressed with how the children looked forward to those gifts and letters. Rather than creating melancholy on those occasions, as David had feared they would, they generated excitement and emotional warmth.

Rachel also had written one letter to David. He obediently waited to open it until the one-year anniversary of her death. In that letter, Rachel told him she knew God had brought them together and blessed them with a wonderful marriage and three beautiful daughters. She told him how much she loved him, that she knew he missed her terribly, and that there would never be another who could replace her in his heart. But she also told him she knew he needed a wife and the girls needed a mother. She asked him to forgive her for not being able to be that wife and mother any more. And she encouraged him to let God lead him to find someone who would appreciate him as the great husband, father, and human being he was, who would love and care for the girls as if they were her own. David was not sure he could ever allow himself to fall in love again. But now, three years later, he had remarried and was making a new life with a very special woman. He had met her while attending a support group for people whose spouses had died.

As he told his personal story at the interfaith breakfast that morning, David noted that at each juncture, at each turning point, God had provided what he needed in order to get through the excruciatingly tough times and to find the life God intended for him after the terrible tragedy of losing Rachel.

"Throughout it all," David said, "I have grown in my capacity to feel the lows and the highs of life, to observe the small miracles present in our lives every day. There was a time, when it became clear to me Rachel was dying and I could do nothing to stop it, when I thought I could never be happy again. But Rachel showed me I was wrong.

"Because of her, I was able to accept not only the reality of her dying but the reality of God's love in the midst of it. I learned that God's reality is so much bigger than the terrible things that happen to us. It includes God's presence with us in our suffering. It is God putting his arms around us and hugging us, and telling us that he too has suffered, and that he loves us more than we can imagine."

David was about to conclude his presentation when his eyes were drawn to a window a few feet to the side of the speaker's stand. Beyond it was a small flower garden, and fluttering in front of the glass was a hummingbird. He watched for a moment while the eyes of his audience followed his. When the hummingbird darted away, David smiled and continued.

"*The road to recovery is paved with moments of grace.* If we have eyes to see, there are moments of transparency when we catch glimpses, in the midst of our sorrows and everyday struggles, that *God is with us, God is for us, and God will never abandon us.* To anyone facing a terrible loss today, my advice is to use your spiritual eyes and see *all* of reality. Moments of grace happen every day."

## *Your Story*

1. Read 2 Corinthians 4:16 and Jeremiah 31:13. Can you identify ways in which God is renewing your spirit each day and working in your life to turn your mourning into gladness?

2. Can you give examples of persons who have reached a state of acceptance in their grieving process? What are the signs that tell you that this milestone has been reached?

3. What do you think the practice of thinking of a happy moment for each day did for David's faith journey? What was your happy moment today?

4. Read Romans 5:3–5. Where have you seen suffering produce perseverance? Perseverance produce character? Character produce hope?

5. The Holy Spirit is our everyday experience of God. Can you think of a recent experience when you have felt God's presence? God's comfort? God's peace?

# DISCOVER NEW MEANING AND PURPOSE

Life-changing events can shatter our dreams and rob us of happiness. For joy to return, we need God's guidance to find new purposes and discover fresh pathways to meaning.

*My days have passed,*
*my plans are shattered,*
*and so are the desires of my heart.*

JOB 17:11


*"I know the plans I have for you," declares the LORD, "plans to*
*prosper you and not to harm you, plans to give you hope and*
*a future."*

JEREMIAH 29:11


*Jesus replied, "'Love the Lord your God with all your heart*
*and with all your soul and with all your mind.' This is the first*
*and greatest commandment. And the second is like it: 'Love*
*your neighbor as yourself.'"*

MATTHEW 22:37–39


*We know that in all things God works for the good of those*
*who love him, who have been called according to his purpose.*

ROMANS 8:28

# 10

# CALLING

### Transforming Your Season of Grieving into a Lifetime of Caring

*Joseph said to them, "Don't be afraid. Am I in the place
of God? You intended to harm me, but God intended it
for good to accomplish what is now being done,
the saving of many lives."*

GENESIS 50:19–20

The gift of acceptance may come rather suddenly and dramatically for some. But for most of us it comes slowly, in bits and pieces over time. Our journeys are not traveled in straight lines. We wander from one stage of grief to another, meandering back and forth and occasionally going in circles. At some point, if we are fortunate, we realize we have arrived at our destination. We may not know exactly when it happened or how we got there, but we have come to experience an inner peace we once believed was impossible to know again.

One of the reasons our journeys are so difficult and slow is that we are not at all sure we *want* to reach acceptance. Even when we are willing to be free of our bitterness and despair, we tend to doubt we ever will come to terms with the terrible things that have happened. We struggle with the notion that it could be right to accept them, and we find it difficult to believe anything good could come from them.

Despite such struggles, if we finally do come to know acceptance, it may be because we have experienced a calling in the midst of our grief that has transformed us from victims of terrible events to agents of change. Such life-altering calls generally come about in one of two ways. The first involves the transformation of anger into a passion for righting the wrongs our personal tragedies have made known to us. The second way is the transformation of our personal sorrow into empathy for those whose agony is similar to our own.

In the first way, passion comes first, followed by empathy. In the second way, empathy comes first, followed by passion. In both cases, the results are similar. We feel called to the work of preventing or alleviating the suffering of others, and when we respond, we set out to make the world a better place. Perhaps unknowingly, we also open ourselves to receive God's healing for our own emotional wounds.

**From Anger to Passion**

As we discussed in chapter 7, anger can be a dangerous emotion. Both for our own sakes and for others, we need to be free from the power and bitterness our resentment has over us. But that does not mean we should banish all feelings of anger on our road to recovery. Anger over tragedies caused by human sin and perversity and over unnecessary suffering due to human ignorance, callousness, or neglect can lead to actions that give meaning to our suffering.

With appropriate intervention, many tragic events can be prevented. And if they cannot be prevented, at least the suffering they produce can be alleviated. We can't respond directly to all the problems and sufferings of the world, but our indignation over a particular form of human suffering can point to a problem God is laying on our hearts for a reason.

In the book of Exodus, we learn that Moses angrily killed an Egyptian who had been beating a Hebrew slave. As a result, Moses fled his privileged life in the household of Pharaoh to the land of Midian, where he lived in exile for decades. But the Bible makes it clear that the plight of his Hebrew brothers and sisters in Egypt, which continued to worsen, weighed heavily on Moses' heart. It is reasonable to assume that his initial anger over the oppression of the Egyptians never fully left him.

In his burning-bush spiritual experience, Moses heard God's call to return to Egypt, a mission that would expose him to great personal danger. Moses answered the call. A journey that began as anger at the treatment of a Hebrew brother resulted in the loss of a privileged life and important relationships. But later that anger and personal tragedy became a calling to free an entire people from the suffering of slavery and to change the course of human events.[24]

In our own time, there are many examples of people who have channeled the righteous anger born of personal suffering into passionate advocacy. Think, for example, of the outraged mother of a child killed by a drunk driver who becomes active in MADD (Mothers Against Drunk Driving) and an advocate in her state for creative sentencing of persons convicted of driving while intoxicated. I once knew a man whose wife was refused treatment at a psychiatric facility because she did not meet the criteria for admission. Within hours of being turned away, she committed suicide. Her incensed husband worked to change the wording of commitment laws in his state so that individuals with symptoms similar to those of his wife would meet the criteria for admission.

Through the actions of such people, the suffering of others often is alleviated or prevented altogether.

### From Sorrow to Empathy

The other avenue that frequently results in a calling to become an agent of change is the transformation of sorrow into empathy. Because we know firsthand what our own suffering is like, we can empathize with the emotional pain of others in similar circumstances. This can be a natural path for those of us whose sadness is so great that we are tempted to despair. Instead of letting ourselves lose hope, we identify with the suffering of others, particularly those going through similar tragic situations.

When we empathize with others, we walk in their shoes. We are able to communicate our identification with their feelings in nonverbal ways.

And when we do speak, we are able to connect with them at a profound level, because we genuinely do feel their pain. When we empathize with the suffering of others, their sense of isolation is overcome. Their burdens become lighter because they no longer feel they must bear them alone. This is one of the reasons support groups of people who have experienced similar losses are so effective in helping each other heal. When members share their similar stories, the fellowship of their suffering becomes a shared source of courage, strength, and hope.

*Whenever our feelings of empathy are strong, we may be receiving a call to serve others.* Empathy can give us the insight and compassion to work for much-needed change. Most of us know or are aware of people who have allowed their personal agony to be transformed through empathy into service and advocacy. For example, we may know someone who decided to enter a medical career after dealing with an injury or illness in the family. Or we may learn from a television program about a wife who became an advocate for funding research to find a cure for the disease that afflicted her husband. There are many such examples.

Some extraordinary people have become famous because of their efforts on behalf of their causes, but most of those who have their grief transformed into a calling are ordinary people who will receive little or no recognition for their efforts. They use their God-given talents and skills as best they can to help bring about change. A calling is not always about a grandiose cause. It may be as simple as taking meals to the sick or transporting others to medical appointments.

Most of us do not answer a call in order to receive recognition but because we desire for the suffering of a loved one not to have been in vain. We want it to mean something. And many of us have found that the best way for this to happen is to discover how our personal losses can help others.

### From Evil to Good

Some losses that occur are so horrific that it is difficult to see how anything constructive can come from them. This may seem especially true when tragic events result from the evil actions of cruel and violent people. Nevertheless, when the suffering of those touched by such events becomes a calling, victims can become God's instruments for transforming evil into good. The biblical stories of Esther and Joseph dramatically illustrate this possibility.

Esther was a Jewish orphan during the time when the Jews were suffering in captivity and exile in Persia. Because of her natural beauty, she was selected by a representative of the king and forced to become a member of the king's harem. In order to survive in that role, she concealed her ethnic identity. The king was impressed with Esther and soon chose her to be his queen.[25]

Later, at the instigation of one of his chief nobles, the king allowed his authority to be used to order the annihilation of the Jewish people. When Esther learned of this, she risked her life by revealing her identity to the king and begged him to intercede on behalf of her people. The king did so, the Jews were spared, and the Jewish annual feast of Purim began.[26]

Joseph, the boy with the coat of many colors in the book of Genesis, was the victim of his brothers' jealousy and hatred. They attacked him and intended to kill him, but due to the intervention of one of the brothers, he was sold into slavery instead.[27]

Many years later, Joseph rose in the ranks of Pharaoh's palace to the position of overseer of the storehouses of grain. When his brothers came to Egypt during a famine to buy food, they were brought before him. The brothers did not recognize Joseph, but he recognized them. When he finally revealed himself to them, they were afraid he would kill them out of revenge. But Joseph forgave them. He told them that their actions were intended to do evil, but God had intended them for good. With those words, Joseph expressed a statement of faith that became a central theme in the Judeo-Christian tradition: *God is able to transform the evil of human beings into God's good work.* For Christians, the greatest symbol of this faith is the crucifixion and resurrection of Jesus.[28]

**Inner Peace**

When our anger turns into passion and our sorrow is transformed into empathy, we may feel a persistent urge to become agents of change. When we answer that call, a strange thing is likely to happen: at some point, while we are engaged in our mission, our inner agony frequently will be replaced by an inner peace. And this will be so even if we remain engaged in an outwardly fierce struggle.

This was certainly my experience. After six years of grieving over my son's illness and struggling to manage his care, something happened in 1984 that changed my life. On a Saturday morning in March, I attended the organizational meeting of the National Alliance on Mental Illness (NAMI) in North Carolina. I listened that day to many other parents of mentally ill children share stories of their struggles and talk about the inadequacies of the state's mental health system of care.

For the first time, I realized how many others were going through the same pain I was experiencing. Through them, God put a great burden on my heart. As I was driving home that evening, I had the most powerful spiritual experience of my life. I felt the presence of God riding with me, and I felt the call of God to become an advocate, not only for my son but for every mentally ill person in the state. The next day I began the work of organizing a NAMI affiliate in my community. Almost immediately, my heart felt lighter and my spirits brighter than they had been in years. And this was only the beginning of what God had in store for my ministry to persons with mental illness.

As people of faith, if we answer our calling and commit our lives to it whenever and however it comes to us, we are able to experience the mysterious activity of our God transforming the evil that has come upon us into his good and loving work.

**Nancy's Story**

Nancy had to fight back the desire to run out of the courtroom and as far away as possible from the men who had raped her and killed her husband and young daughter. But under the guidance of the prosecutor, Nancy told the court her story.

At 8:30 on a weeknight, after the dishes were done and three-year-old Keri had been put to bed, Nancy and her husband, Carl, settled down to watch television in the family room. The doorbell rang, and Nancy went to the door. As she started to open it, two men dressed in dark clothes pushed in the door and knocked her backwards. One of them grabbed Nancy. She screamed. Carl came running and was confronted by the two men, one with a gun. He ordered Carl to sit down while the other tied him up. Then they forced him to watch as they raped his wife, taking turns assaulting her before they casually took a break and raided the refrigerator. They found a couple of bottles of wine and drank them. When Nancy tried to untie Carl, the man now on trial grabbed a butcher knife and attacked her. Critically injured, Nancy collapsed to the floor and lost consciousness; then the man stabbed and killed Carl.

Nancy could not provide direct testimony for what happened next, but police detectives had learned the rest of the story. The two men then went through the house, looking for valuables. They found some change in a jar in the master bedroom closet. They took some of Nancy's costume jewelry. They never found her expensive jewelry. But they did find Carl and Nancy's daughter Keri. They put tape over Keri's mouth. They wrapped her in a blanket and took her with them as they left the house near midnight.

A neighbor walking his dog saw the two men struggling to carry a bundle while running to a car. Alarmed, he dialed 911 and reported the incident. When the police arrived, they discovered that, miraculously, Nancy still had a pulse. An ambulance arrived a few minutes later. Nancy almost died that night.

The community organized a massive effort to find little Keri. They systematically searched local parks, vacant lots, and several wooded sections on the outskirts of town. They posted pictures of Keri on light poles and in store windows. Three television stations carried photos of the three-year-old and asked for the public's assistance. The faith communities held candlelight vigils and started prayer chains. But Keri could not be found.

The neighbor who had called the police had managed to remember part of a license plate number and describe the car. One match turned out to be a car registered to a felon who previously had been convicted of armed robbery and rape. Only six weeks before the assault in Nancy's home, this man had been released from prison even though he had been scheduled to serve many more years, because the prosecutor who had convicted him had committed prosecutorial misconduct in an unrelated trial. As a result of the misconduct case, eight persons previously convicted in separate cases were released pending retrials.

Eventually police identified and arrested the second attacker as well. The two men had seen Nancy in the grocery store and followed her home, determining to return that night. Police reached a plea agreement with the second attacker, taking the death penalty off the table in return for his full confession, testimony against the accused, and information leading to the recovery of Keri's remains. After the agreement was signed, he led authorities to the location of a shallow grave in a field. Two days later, the community turned out in large numbers for Keri's funeral, to express their sympathy to Nancy and their outrage at the perpetrators.

When the second attacker took the stand, he confirmed Nancy's version of the events of the evening and testified it was the accused who had murdered Carl and Keri. Forensic evidence dramatically supported the testimony that the two men had been in the house where the crime took place. DNA tests verified that the skin scrapings under Nancy's fingernails belonged to the accused. The jury took less than four hours to return a verdict of guilty. A day later, after the penalty hearing, the jury recommended the death penalty. The judge formalized their recommendation by sentencing the attacker to death by lethal injection.

Nancy had hoped to feel some closure when the trial was over. She was not sure what that would feel like, but she had heard others speak of it. And she did feel a little safer. She found she could sleep through an entire night without waking up in fear. She had hoped the results of the trial also would bring some kind of inward satisfaction that would allow her to feel less pain. But that did not happen.

As Nancy soon realized, the failure to experience the healing she longed for had nothing to do with the fact that it would take many years before the sentence was carried out. She now understood that even if the execution of the man who had raped her and murdered her child and husband were to take place immediately, the relief she desperately longed for would not come because it could not bring back Keri and Carl. Nothing would ever be the same again.

Nancy had spent much of the year leading up to the trial filled with rage toward her attackers. After the trial, her anger settled into a bitter resentment accompanied by depression. She had read somewhere about stages of grieving and that people eventually are supposed to reach a state of acceptance. She doubted that would be possible for her. She thought she might be one of the people who get stuck in their anger and depression and never reach acceptance. She felt she could never accept the unimaginable things that had happened to her and her loved ones.

She remembered having been taught as a child that God works in all things for good, but she could not believe any good could come out of such a horror. She realized she was not angry with her attackers alone, but she was also deeply and profoundly angry with God for not intervening. If faith cannot provide protection from unspeakable evil, she reasoned, then what good is it?

But when Nancy next knelt by the graves of her husband and daughter, she found herself unable to resist the urge to turn once more to God. She was not looking for answers to the mystery of evil in the world, or why terrible things happen to people which are completely out of proportion to any wrong they have ever done. She knew in her heart, after what she had been through, that no explanation could ever be adequate. But she also knew she could not give up on God, because she needed God that morning. She could not face the future without Carl and Keri without help from a Power greater than herself.

Nancy realized at the cemetery that the anger and resentment she still harbored toward the attackers was eating her up inside. She did not want to forgive them, and she did not want God to forgive them. She wanted them to rot in hell. But now that the trial was over, she also longed to be free of the evil that had fallen upon her family. She realized that as long as she was consumed with hatred toward her attackers, their evil still had as much power over her as it had the night they held her down and raped her. As long as she feared and hated them, she was still their victim. She would never know closure without acceptance, and acceptance was not possible without forgiveness.

Reluctantly, Nancy prayed for God to help her find enough forgiveness to release her from her prison of hatred and resentment. And she prayed God would move the mountain of her despair and give her hope and peace again. She did not feel much confidence that God would answer her prayers. Her lack of faith was much greater than the little bit of faith remaining in her heart. But she remembered Jesus' saying that even if someone's faith is only the size of a tiny seed, it could still move mountains. In the midst of her prayers, Nancy felt a sudden urge to stand up and look around the cemetery.

As she surveyed the burial sites stretching in all directions, she became curiously aware of many crosses in various shapes, styles, and sizes. She thought about Jesus' suffering and dying on the cross. At that moment, the realization that God had not intervened to save Jesus from an awful death pressed itself on her mind. She had believed, as long as she could remember, that Jesus died for our sins, but she now began to understand for the first time what he had gone through on that cross. And she remembered and was comforted by the words he had cried out: "My God, my God, why have you forsaken me?" Jesus must have felt that day exactly as she was feeling now—forsaken by the Father.

Nancy recalled how at the death of Jesus, darkness had come over the whole land. It occurred to her that she had been going through the season of her own personal time of darkness. She left the graves that day with a spark of hope in her heart for a new season, the season of the resurrection of her own spirit. She wanted again to take charge of her life.

She wanted the stone rolled away so she could come out of the tomb of her own despair. There must be a reason why she had not died along with her husband and daughter, but what? Was there something she was supposed to do with her life so that evil would not have the last word?

The spiritual resurrection Nancy hoped for did not come through some dramatic religious insight or experience but through the most mundane of ways. A few days later, as she watched a TV talk show, the topic of everyday heroes grabbed her attention. This was a program about people who had been through personal suffering and who had found in that suffering a calling to service. Nancy watched and listened carefully.

Some of the heroes on the program were people whose experiences were similar to her own. They also had been victims of violent crimes. One man, for example, had been severely disabled when he was shot during a convenience-store robbery. Another ordinary hero was a rape survivor. Nancy learned that many of the important laws passed in various states and nationally over the past few decades were the result of someone turning personal tragedy into something good. Despite the reality that some tragedies are more horrible than others, Nancy realized upon reflection that suffering is suffering. It hurts no matter how it comes about. But she also recognized that most suffering people need to identify with others who have shared a kind of suffering similar to their own. Most of those on the program had attempted to reach out to help people much like themselves. A comment one of the heroes made especially struck home that day. "I knew if I sat at home and allowed resentment and anger to fester, or felt sorry for myself and decided life was not worth living, evil would win. I could not let that happen."

Nancy knew what she had to do. She had to seek God's help in *transforming her own season of grieving into a lifetime of caring.* She began to watch the news and to make personal contacts with others who had been victims of crimes. Later she organized support groups for violent-crime victims and their families, and she set up a Web-based support chat room.

Nancy remembered that the crime that had destroyed her family could have been prevented if a prosecutor had not been guilty of misconduct. He had proceeded to trial in a capital case while intentionally concealing clear evidence of an accused man's innocence, and the state bar concluded the prosecutor had done this because he believed a guilty verdict would help him win an upcoming election. Despite the seriousness of the offense, the prosecutor's law license had been suspended for just one year; he had not violated any existing criminal law. Nancy fought to change that. She went to the legislature again and again until legislation was passed providing criminal penalties for prosecutors who deliberately failed to follow the rules of discovery.

In the process, Nancy experienced healing. Somehow the deaths of her husband and child had meaning. Nothing would ever be as it was before, but Nancy now participated in the reality that evil does not have the final victory. She felt within her being that God had taken the horrific evil unleashed on her family and somehow transformed it into good. Because of the tragedy and her response to it, others were being comforted in their suffering, and some future tragedies were being prevented.

One Sunday morning, at the request of her minister, Nancy witnessed to her faith during morning worship. As she concluded her talk, she said, "I do not know any more today than I did then why God does not always prevent evil from happening. I have stopped worrying about that. What I know from experience is that God weeps when I weep. God suffers when I suffer. And somehow, mysteriously, God works in me, and in so very many others who know life's tragedies, to turn suffering into service and evil into good.

"When our Lord taught us to pray 'Deliver us from evil,' I think he expected us to put legs on that prayer. He expected us to give our very best to that struggle. As I have studied the Bible and watched the news, I have come to understand that God often looks around for some ordinary person who has experienced profound suffering and calls that person to the work of transforming evil into good. It is not that God calls and then abandons us as we take up the task. Not by any stretch of the imagination. Psalm 22 begins with the words Jesus quoted on the cross, 'My God, my God, why have you forsaken me?' But it does not end here. Later on in that psalm, we also find these words: 'For he has not despised or disdained the suffering of the afflicted one; he has not hidden his face from him but has listened to his cry for help' (Ps. 22:24).

"God does not abandon us in our suffering, and he does not abandon us in our mission. God calls us, and through his presence, power, compassion, healing, and leading, we are able to do far more than we ever could have imagined. And so I ask all of you who have been struck by some type of tragedy in your own lives to hear God's promise to his people today: 'We know that all things work together for good for those who love God, who are called according to his purpose'" (Rom. 8:28 NRSV).

## *Your Story*

1. Read Genesis 50:19–20. God turned the evil intentions of Joseph's brothers into good. Can you think of modern examples where God has transformed evil into good?

2. Have you ever felt that it would be a betrayal of someone you loved to forgive another person? Why do you think Nancy eventually prayed for God to help her forgive the two men despite her reluctance to do so?

3. Can you give examples of everyday heroes who turned suffering into service? Do you think a person who touches only a few lives is any less of a hero than someone who champions a major cause,?

4. Read Romans 8:28. What experience with suffering have you had that God can use for good? When has God already done that?

5. Read Isaiah 6:8 and Matthew 22:37–39. Specifically, what service is God calling you to today?

# 11

# AFFIRMATION

## When the Caterpillar Dies, the Butterfly Flies

*I have learned the secret of being content in any and every
situation, whether well fed or hungry, whether living
in plenty or in want. I can do everything through him
who gives me strength."*
PHILIPPIANS 4:12–13

In the *Peanuts* cartoon created by Charles Schultz, Charlie Brown's favorite expression was always "Good grief!" Upon reflection, this exclamation might seem a strange combination of words. In light of a world filled with tragedies, we may ask, "How can something caused by a terrible loss and accompanied by painful feelings ever be positive? How can grief be good?" Yet as we have seen in previous chapters, if we have accepted and lived our own journey of grief as part of our journey of faith, we have had glimpses of the goodness of grief all along the way.

Grief can be good because it softens the blow and eases our pain until such time as we are better able to cope with it. Grief releases the intense emotional pressure within that threatens to do long-term damage to our emotions and bodies. Grief forces us to struggle for a time with our questions, our anger, our guilt, and our sorrow so that we might reach the day when we will be free from their power over us. Grief can be good because it sensitizes us to the suffering of others, awakens empathy, and calls us to respond in service to the needs of our neighbors. And no matter how horrific a tragedy is, grief can become the means whereby God transforms evil in this world into good.

At a profoundly personal level, grief also can be good because it leads us to a more mature faith and deeper spiritual experience, transforming our anxieties about living into genuine contentment and guiding us toward living each day in the reality that *God is good all the time.*

## Contentment

If we can see our journeys of grief through eyes of faith, we will see important lessons to be learned. For example, as we saw with Rachel in chapter 2, *our experiences of grief can teach us that our external situations are never our problem. Our problem is always to be found in the relationships we have with them.*

Every difficulty confronts us with choices, whether we are conscious of them or not:

"What is my attitude toward this going to be?"

"Will I be resentful, bitter, and cynical?"

"Or will I be humble, grateful, and life affirming?"

"Will I focus on the negatives and limitations, or will I look for the positives and possibilities?"

As the apostle Paul faced persecutions and hardships, he understood that his situation was never his problem. His relationship with Jesus Christ gave him the gift of contentment no matter what was going on in his life. If he was well-fed, that was fine, of course. If he was hungry, that was no problem either. Paul had received the grace to be content with or without the comforts of life, and he desired that the believers in the churches he had founded would also have that same contentment in the midst of their circumstances.

*No matter how difficult and tragic our situations, our attitudes make a difference.* Those who have survived concentration camps and prisoner-of-war camps have testified that survival under such horrible conditions often depends on people's attitudes. Those who continue to have faith and hold fast to their hopes, and who are able to be compassionate toward others, are more likely to survive. And those who do not survive but who have possessed these same attitudes can help to make survival possible for others.

Another lesson grief has to teach us is that there is no need to "sweat the small stuff." Because tragedy separates us from someone or something precious to us, it can help us focus on what is truly important in life. It can put into perspective the little daily aggravations of life. It can help us see the humor in our situations rather than lose our serenity because someone or something has thwarted our self-will. And it may assist us in detaching from our preoccupation with material possessions and self-centered pleasure to refocus on our relationships.

The loss of a parent, for example, may leave us lonely and longing for his or her company once again, but it also may motivate us to put more emphasis on spending quality time with our living loved ones. And it may compel us to focus on the reality of the way life is. In a few years, if not before, we too will die, as will all of our loved ones. As far as this world is concerned, we are, as the book of James says, "a mist that appears for a little while and then vanishes" (James 4:14). This awareness of mortality may help us see every moment of life as a precious gift.

The death of a parent also may remind us that life is seasonal. It begins with the springtime of childhood and youth, continues through the summer of adulthood, the fall of mature years, and the winter of old age and death. Of course, death may come at any point along the way. But if we continue in each season, we are confronted with the question of the meaning and purpose of that season.

Each season of life holds new and difficult challenges. Our family and work responsibilities usually shift over time. For people of faith, our particular roles as servants of God may change as well. Sometimes we try to resist life's transitions. Yet we are given the choice to embrace the change and know contentment or resist the change and miss the banquet that life is.

**Purpose**

The psalmist tells us that after the long, dark night of weeping, joy comes with the morning light.[29] Dawn is the end of the night, but it also is the beginning of a new day. And every morning confronts us with decisions about what we are going to do with the gift of the day before us.

All periods of significant change are stressful times. This is so even when the change is a happy one, such as when a child is born. Much of our stress is rooted in the reality that major changes in our life situations usually require us to change as well. *When we encounter such turning points, we may find ourselves in need of discovering new purposes and new roles.* This is especially true when we must start over after we have lost persons or circumstances that previously helped to define us and what our lives were about. For example, some of us have spent months and even years providing care to loved ones. Our caretaking may have defined, for the most part, our reason for being. After our loved ones are gone and no longer need our help, we may feel unsure about our roles in the universe. At such times, it is not unusual for us to feel a bit lost. People whose lives previously focused on making money and accumulating wealth and possessions also may feel the need to find new reasons for living after experiencing loss and a period of grief. Their old goals now feel empty and meaningless. They long for a fresh life direction that will make them genuinely happy and fulfilled.

If we are people of faith, our general purpose is clear. We are each, as Jesus indicated, to love God with our whole heart, mind, and strength, and our neighbors as ourselves.[30] To be about the love of God and neighbor is why we were created. That, of course, is what Jesus himself did. He went about being the love for God, and the love of God, in the world. And with the aid of the Holy Spirit, that is what we too are supposed to do with our lives.

Grief does not change our general purpose as people of faith, but it may challenge us to rethink what our individual and unique purposes might be. While for some this involves a particular personal calling, for many of us it has more to do with recognizing the gifts we have been given, even when they are modest ones. And it means deciding each day to be open to using our talents according to God's general purpose.

Furthermore, because of life changes, we may face new circumstances that prevent us from being faithful servants in the same ways as before. We can be faithful servants nonetheless. A man who is housebound with a disability, for example, may not be able to be involved in the construction projects of Habitat for Humanity as in the past. But he still may be able to use his computer to help with the organization's record keeping, fund raising, and publicity. A woman who once gave significant sums of money to her church and to charities may not have the resources to continue that support. But she still may be able to provide substantial service to those organizations by donating her time and using her skills to help carry out their missions. A retired couple with health problems may no longer be able to participate in church and civic activities. But they still may be able to participate in their church's prayer chain and spend time each day in prayer for others. Even an elderly man bedridden in a nursing home can do more than wait to die. He can decide to see each encounter with nursing staff and visitors as an opportunity to show appreciation and offer encouragement. And this can be done with a wink or a smile even when he is too weak to speak. For as long as we have conscious life, we have the ability to allow God's love to flow through us to others.

## Joy

When we have reached the dawn of acceptance, we face a new day. In fact, it is likely that we face many new days. And those days will pass, whether we live them as people of faith and according to God's purposes for our lives or not. If we have learned the lessons God wants us to learn as we have gone through the agonizing stages of our grief, acceptance has become for us far more than resignation or even a calling. It has matured into the grace to embrace life as it comes to us each day. And it is the assurance that God is good all the time, even when it does not feel that way.

When we are in the midst of our journeys of grief, we may feel we will never know joy again. Yet many who have walked before us through the valley of sorrow testify to the reality that joy will return if we allow it to. If we have eyes to see, there are happy moments in each day and times of joy in each season of life.

But for people of faith, joy is much more than this. The apostle Paul wrote of a boundless joy in the midst of his troubles. Joy is a feeling we possess in our hearts at all times, even when we are having the most difficult of days. It does not depend on the successful pursuit of pleasure or material things. It is not conditioned upon whether life is going the way we wish it would.

The joy of our faith is a durable joy. It dwells within us at all times because God's love dwells within us. It is a taste of that perfect joy we will know in the life to come. Death never can defeat us. Suffering and sorrow will end. And nothing ever will separate us from the love of God.

## Alice's Story

Despite their modest retirement savings, Alice and her husband, Ed, retired early in order to spend time together. They moved from the large four-bedroom home where their three sons had grown to maturity into a two-bedroom house in a retirement community. For two years they enjoyed wonderful traveling adventures together. They visited Italy, took a Caribbean cruise, spent two weeks in Hawaii, and drove to a variety of places where they could enjoy the beauty of nature and entertaining events. Then Ed had a stroke and died.

Ed's passing understandably devastated Alice. They had married when she was only nineteen and had remained together for forty-two years. They were not only husband and wife but also best friends. They enjoyed each other's company so much that they had little time or need to socialize with others.

Those two years of retirement had been magnificent. Despite her grief over Ed's death, Alice was very grateful to God for them. But after losing him, she felt lost. She felt her own life was over. So much of her identity had been tied up with his that she did not feel like a person anymore. She felt empty and useless.

Alice and Ed's three sons each lived hundreds of miles away and had families of their own. After Ed's passing, Alice spent a week at each of their homes. All three sons and their families were pleasant enough, but during the visits Alice felt like a fifth wheel. As she flew home from the final visit, she wondered if it might have been more comfortable for her if one of her children had been a daughter. The visits had underscored the reality that her children had busy lives of their own. She knew future visits would be short and far between.

Alice had not been home more than a few days when she received a call that her mother, who lived in an assisted-living community, had fallen, broken her hip, and was in the hospital. Alice rushed to her side. After the surgery, Alice was told that her mother would not be able to return to her previous residence because she needed rehabilitation therapy and skilled nursing care. So upon her mother's release from the hospital, Alice arranged for her mother to be transferred to a nursing home near her own retirement community.

Over the next few months, Alice spent most of her waking hours at the nursing home. Her mother was ninety-two years of age; the fall and the surgery had weakened her already frail body. She was not able to get out of bed without being lifted and positioned by nursing staff. That activity was so painful for her that she soon refused their assistance, preferring to be bedridden. To make matters worse, an inflammation around the surgical wound was determined to be a treatment-resistant infection.

Alice's mother now needed considerable assistance with her personal needs. And so Alice spent long and exhausting days as a caregiver. Sometimes when her mother was sleeping, Alice escaped to a peaceful garden courtyard in search of a moment of serenity. There she came to know Grace, who was married to a man receiving care in the Alzheimer's wing of the nursing home. Although Grace was a few years older than Alice, the two women were drawn to each other's friendship. Over the weeks, they found themselves looking forward to those moments of respite when they could sit outside on a bench together and chat about happier times.

Despite Alice's dedicated and loving care and that of nursing staff, Alice's mother grew weaker every day. Her pain grew more severe. Six months after her fall, she developed pneumonia and had to be transported by ambulance to a local hospital. She continued to decline, and eight days after being taken to the hospital, with Alice faithfully beside her bed, she slipped into a coma.

During those difficult six months at the nursing facility, Alice's pastor had been diligent about visiting at least weekly and praying with mother and daughter. During the hospitalization he visited every other day. When her mother slipped into a coma, Alice called the pastor, and within an hour he arrived. Pastor Phil took her mother's small hand and spoke to her as if she were fully awake. "You are in a great position today," he said. "Maybe God will make you better, and you can spend a little more time here with this precious daughter you brought into the world, this one you love so very much and who loves you just as much in return. Or perhaps God will take you away from her, and you can go to the other side, and you can be with all those loved ones who have gone before you. And there, all of you will rejoice because you have been reunited. Isn't that great? You are a winner either way." Then Pastor Phil offered a moving prayer while tears streaked Alice's cheeks.

A few hours after Pastor Phil left, Alice could hear her mother's breathing become labored and erratic. That night, as Alice sat quietly holding her hand, she felt her mother slipping away. The breathing stopped. The suffering finally was over.

Alice sat for a long time before she notified the night shift. She was exhausted, deeply sad, and guiltily relieved. She tried not to think of what her own life was going to be like, now that her mother did not need her care anymore.

All three of Alice's sons flew in to attend the funeral, though they all decided to leave their busy families at home. Alice sat with her children and listened as Pastor Phil read the Scriptures, prayed, and offered his words of comfort and strength. Pastor Phil, as usual, had a lot of good things to say that day. But the words that meant the most to Alice were the ones about the caterpillar and the butterfly.

"There is something ahead finer than we can dream of," the pastor said. "If a lowly caterpillar could talk as he makes his way over twigs and stones, he would ridicule the idea that before long he will be a multicolored butterfly, floating easily from flower to flower. But we know that when the caterpillar dies, the butterfly flies. He is changed from one kind of life and being to a very different and more glorious kind of being. In a similar way, when our earthly phase is finished, God transforms us into our next phase, into a wondrous and glorious new being."

Alice thought about those earlier, happier times when she had enjoyed watching the butterflies in her mother's flower garden. Her mother had loved butterflies. Alice also remembered enjoying the butterflies in the courtyard garden of the nursing home. Alice found great comfort in the pastor's words.

But as Alice tried to get back to a normal life, she found herself perpetually perplexed. She did not know what *normal* was supposed to be anymore. After all, normal once had been raising the boys, working as a bookkeeper at a local hardware store, and being a good wife. After retirement, normal was spending every possible moment with Ed. Then normal meant spending every possible moment providing care for her mother after her fall.

Now that she was alone again, Alice felt empty and useless. To make matters worse, she began to develop some health problems of her own. In the midst of these difficulties, Alice could not get the images of her mother's decline out of her mind. One day a great sorrow came over her like a tidal wave. She wept for hours until she cried herself to sleep. Alice had shed a lot of tears over the past months and years, but this was different. Her sorrow was not about losing what had been but about the losses to come. Her mother's journey through old age, sickness, and death had given Alice a profound visualization of her own future.

Someone at the nursing home had a sign on the wall that read, "Old

age is not for sissies." *How true!* Alice thought now. She understood that
she had wept deeply about her life because she was experiencing a tragic
awareness of her own mortality. *I hope that when the time comes, I go suddenly,* she thought. *I don't know if I can stand to go through what my mother
went through.*

Grace and Alice had been getting together for dinner on Thursday
evenings. Grace could not help but notice Alice's darker-than-usual
mood when they met at the restaurant after Alice's mother died. In her
usual soft, caring voice, Grace gently asked, "What's going on? You don't
look like you feel so well."

"It shows that much, does it?" Alice responded. "I think I'm OK, but I'm
depressed, and I just feel so lost. I miss Ed. I miss my boys. I miss Mom.
And I just feel useless. My life used to have a purpose. Now I only exist.
I feel like I'm just getting up and going through the motions every day. I
don't want to be like this, but I don't know how to change it. You seem to
be handling things pretty well, all things considered. How do you do it?"

"You have been through a lot lately, so don't be so hard on yourself
for being in the dumps," Grace replied. "Some days I wake up and think
about what has happened to my life and to my husband, and I can hardly
get through the day. But most days I remember that I must still be here
for a reason. So I try to take it one day at a time and see if I can figure out
why the Lord has given me that day."

"I felt some of that when I was still taking care of Mom," Alice said.
"But now that she's gone, I don't seem to have a purpose anymore. Life is
hard. Nothing really brings me much joy. All I can think about is that I
am getting older and older and more useless all the time—"

"Just listen to yourself!" Grace interrupted. "That is quite a pity pot
you are sitting on. Look, you may not be as healthy as you used to be.
None of us are. You may have lost your mother and your husband. But
you still have family, even if they live a long way from here. You still have
your life, and you haven't lost your mind like my husband has. So maybe
it's time for you to figure out what God wants you to do with this season
of your life besides sit around and wait to die of old age."

Alice was stunned. It was the first time Grace had spoken anything other than kind, gentle words. She knew Grace was right. But she just didn't know how to do anything about it.

"I don't think I have anything to offer anymore," Alice said. "I don't have any real talents. The only things I ever have been good at were balancing books, taking care of my children, being a good wife to Ed, and being a good daughter to my mother."

"Nonsense! You have a lot to offer. Have you ever considered some type of volunteer service?"

"I know a lot of people my age volunteer to be leaders in the church or in other kinds of groups. But that is just not who I am. I never have been good at that sort of thing. I know some people have hobbies, like painting pictures and making quilts, but I don't have any hobbies. I suppose I should think about volunteering to help out at the nursing home, but I don't think my nerves could stand it now that Mom is gone. It would be too depressing for me. I think I am a pretty useless human being."

Returning to her usual comforting tone, Grace replied, "Nobody says you have to do any of those things. Let's see if we can figure out what God might have in mind for you now. Remember when you were young? God's first assignment was for you to grow into maturity, to get a good education, to develop character and compassion, and to be a good daughter and friend. Would you agree?"

Alice nodded.

"In the next phase of life, God's assignment was for you to be a good wife to Ed and a good mother to your children. You were faithful to Ed and supported him in what he did, as he was faithful to love and support you. You also had the assignment of delivering your children to adulthood and maturity as individuals who would be self-supporting, good citizens, as those who would know and serve God and make a positive contribution to the world."

"I never thought of it that way before."

"From what you've told me, in the third season, while you continued to grow in your relationship with Ed, you became a bookkeeper at a hardware store, and you had the assignment to be an honest and good employee who made a contribution to that business while saving for your retirement with Ed."

Alice nodded again.

"Then in the most recent season of your life, you were taken on a roller coaster. First you had the gift of joy, sharing wonderful experiences with your husband. Then you had the assignment to care for your elderly and infirm mother. Do you think that pretty much describes what God's plan has been for you till now?"

"Yes, I guess that pretty much sums up my life."

"Now, I suspect you have entered a new period," Grace continued. "So what does God have in mind for you? Look, you say you have no talent and nothing to offer. But look at what you offered others all those years. You seem to have handled those assignments in excellent fashion. The common thread of what your life has been about over the years is your family. And now I believe you have something else to offer your family, something that only someone of your age and experience *can* offer."

"And what, pray tell, is that?"

"Wisdom. You have wisdom. And your children and grandchildren need that wisdom. You know one of the things I think is wrong with our culture? We don't honor the wisdom of those with age and experience. In some cultures, when you get gray hair, you are honored. The elders are considered the keepers of the wisdom necessary for the good of the tribe or community. Our society, on the other hand, worships youth and inexperience. But that doesn't mean we should submit to that foolishness and keep silent."

"I'm not sure where you are going with this, Grace."

"Don't you see? When we get old, we may not have the strength or health to contribute the way we were able to when we were younger. But we have knowledge and wisdom the next generations need. And it is our assignment from God to see that they get it."

"So you think I should become some kind of meddling old fool?"

"Oh no! Not at all! What you need is to determine some ways that will communicate your wisdom effectively, so the next generations will have it when they need it or when they are able to appreciate it, even if that's after you're gone."

"So how do I do that?"

"Well, let's start with this. What do your children and grandchildren know about their family heritage? What do they really know about you and Ed and what life was like before they were born? Do you have any old family pictures?"

"Boxes of them. Some were Mom's and some were from Ed's family. And lots are from when our kids were growing up."

"And what do you think will happen to all those precious pictures after you are gone?"

"They probably will be stored in somebody's home, or they could be lost or destroyed. I doubt if the boys will recognize many of the people in the old pictures."

"Well," Grace asked, "don't you think your family needs to have those pictures in a format that will allow them to understand and experience their heritage?"

As Alice drove home and prepared for bed, she felt an excitement for the first time in a long time. There just might be a purpose for her life after all. As she lay awake thinking about the evening's conversation and her role as keeper of the family heritage, she resolved first to have all the family pictures converted to digital images so they could be preserved on disk. Then she would sort them and arrange them into photo albums, labeling and identifying the people and places in the pictures and when they were taken. Then it occurred to her that no one had yet put together a genealogical record of the family. She would need to get started on that too. There were family stories her father and mother had told her, and stories she had to tell of her own childhood and youth. These were interesting snippets from the past, and some of the stories contained life lessons learned the hard way and worth sharing.

Sometime in the middle of the night, when Alice got up to go to the bathroom, she found herself thinking about writing a book to record those family stories. Then her children and grandchildren could learn about their heritage. *When they're ready, when the time is right,* she thought, *they'll want to know. And it is my assignment to make sure their heritage is not lost.* Because the book would be of interest only to the family, she knew it would need to be self-published. But that would be a good use for the small inheritance she had received from her mother's estate. There was so much to do now! Alice was worried there might not be enough time to do it all.

Many years later, when Alice was bedridden in the same nursing home that had cared for her mother, her oldest son sat by her side. While she was sleeping, he noticed a book sitting next to a stack of photo albums on the dresser, with a blue cover adorned with a large image of a black-and-yellow butterfly. He opened the book and read the introduction:

At my mother's funeral, my pastor spoke of the transformation of a caterpillar to a butterfly. He spoke of this as a symbol of the change from life in this world to eternal life. The image represents that change for me as well. But the butterfly also reminds me of the changes required of each of us as we advance through the seasons of life that God has appointed for us.

In each season, God has assignments for us, no matter what our condition. In my golden years, God assigned me the joyful responsibility to pass to you, my children and grandchildren, the stories that will help you know how life was lived by those who came before you and how you came to be who you are today. In doing this, I have tried to pass along some of the wisdom I learned from those who are no longer with us.

If you will read this book and let the pictures, stories, and sayings of those who gave you life live in your hearts, they will richly bless your lives. I pray each of you will find God's purpose for you at each season of your life. And when you get old, as I have gotten old, you will know that as long as you are still here, God is not through with you yet. And if, as you read this book, you think God is through with me, don't be too sure. I can't wait to find out what my assignment will be in heaven.

## *Your Story*

1.  Read Philippians 4:12–13. What is contentment? What circumstances challenge your contentment these days?
2.  A life-changing loss can cause us to rethink our priorities in life. What do you want your priorities to be for the foreseeable future?
3.  Alice described herself after the death of her mother as useless. What would you say to those who believe they are useless and have nothing to offer?
4.  Read Ecclesiastes 3:1. Alice embraced her golden years' assignment as the keeper and communicator of the family heritage and wisdom. What do you think might be God's assignment for you in your current season of life?
5.  Read Revelation 7:15–17. If you can imagine God having an assignment for you in heaven, what might that be?

# Epilogue

More than three decades have gone by since my son's onset of schizophrenia. During the first several years, Mark was trapped in a revolving door between home and psychiatric hospitals. Local, appropriate, community-based services were virtually nonexistent for those with Mark's diagnosis.

As I described in chapter 10, in 1984 I attended a state organizational meeting of the National Alliance on Mental Illness (NAMI). As I drove home from that meeting, I felt that I was being called to a ministry of advocacy, and I soon threw myself into the work of NAMI. I served as the executive director of the organization for six years before going to work for my state's Division of Mental Health, Developmental Disabilities and Substance Abuse Services.

NAMI helped to bring attention to the problems of persons with serious mental illness in our state, and in time, community services began to appear. Eventually, the impact on Mark's life was dramatic. He would have other crises. But he also had long periods of stability. At the time of this writing, he has experienced only two brief hospitalizations during the past fifteen years and is participating in the benefits of services primarily made possible by NAMI advocacy.

Through the years since the onset of my son's mental illness, I have experienced several other life-changing times of grief. The final year of the last millennium was a particularly tough one. The responsibility of being the director of a state service system hampered by inadequate resources to serve the needs of its clients, and with never-ending governmental turbulence, was by nature a difficult assignment. But in 1999, it was especially so, due largely, I believe, to political circumstances beyond my control. More significantly, it was a profoundly sad year for my family. My mother was diagnosed with cancer and died five months later. Mark caught his hand in a wood splitter and had to have it reattached. My father-in-law, who was also my close friend, dropped dead of a heart attack. My dear mother-in-law declined rapidly in health after the death of her husband and, a few months later, also passed away. More recently, in 2012, while I was preparing this book for publication, my lovely wife, Diane, was diagnosed with uterine cancer and underwent major surgery. (At this writing she is still recovering and has been given a good prognosis.)

These experiences and the other seasons of grief I have known along the way have not been nearly as difficult, however, as the early years of Mark's mental illness. I believe that is true largely because God has changed me over the years, as God has changed the lives of countless other people of faith who also have faced personal tragedies.

For me and for the people who inspired the writing of this book, life-changing tragedies offer the opportunity, however painful, for faith to mature and deepen. When naïve faith no longer can serve as a kind of talisman to ward off bad experiences, authentic faith calls us to live in God's real world and to accept and affirm the reality of our suffering. God does not prevent bad things from happening to people of faith. But God does abide with us, and God does suffer with us, when such things happen. Our journeys through the dark shadows are paved with moments of grace if we have eyes to see them. And, mysteriously, God is able to transform the evil that befalls us into good if we open ourselves to his guidance. In faith we are assured that no matter what else befalls us, God is for us, God is with us, and God will never abandon us.

My hope and prayer is that this book will help you on *your* journey of faith, to affirm with me the words of the psalmist, "The LORD is close to the brokenhearted and saves those who are crushed in spirit" (Ps. 34:18).

# NOTES

1. From "How Firm a Foundation," Robert Keene, 1787
2. Amos 5:11, 18; 6:1; Isaiah 28:14–15
3. Psalm 23
4. 2 Samuel 12
5. Exodus 2:11–15; 3:1–10; 1 Kings 18:16–19:18
6. Luke 9:28–36
7. Genesis 3:1–10
8. John 5:6
9. Luke 15:11–31
10. Luke 23:34
11. Luke 22:42
12. Mark 15:34
13. See Job 3:11; 7:20; 9:29
14. Matthew 5:45
15. Job 1
16. See Amos 5:22–24 as an Old Testament example; John 2:13–16
17. Luke 13:4–5
18. Job 6:8–9; Genesis 4:1–8
19. 2 Samuel 18:33; Jeremiah 9:1; Luke 19:41; Matthew 26:75; John 20:11
20. Genesis 19:15–26
21. Genesis 50:19–20; Romans 8:28
22. Genesis 19:15–26
23. From Psalm 30:5; from Keene, "How Firm a Foundation"
24. Exodus 2:11–15; 3:1–10
25. Esther 1:1–2:18
26. Esther 2:19–9:32
27. Genesis 37:1–28

28. Genesis 50:15–21; Romans 8:28; Luke 23:44–46; 24:5–6
29. Psalm 30:5
30. Matthew 22:37–39

# ABOUT THE AUTHOR

Rev. Dr. John F. Baggett is a graduate of Kentucky Wesleyan College and Vanderbilt Divinity School. He holds a master's in the anthropology of religion, and a PhD in psychiatric anthropology from the University of North Carolina at Chapel Hill. He has served United Methodist pastorates in Kentucky, Tennessee, and Chicago, and has been a frequent lecturer in theology, biblical studies, and anthropology.

In midlife John was called to a new ministry on behalf of mentally ill persons and their families. He has served as the executive director of the National Alliance for the Mentally Ill of North Carolina and as the director of the North Carolina Division of Mental Health, Developmental Disabilities and Substance Abuse Services. In addition to numerous mental health and religious articles, John is the author of *Seeing Through the Eyes of Jesus: His Revolutionary View of Reality and His Transcendent Significance for Faith* (Eerdmans, 2008).

John and his wife, Diane—a professional grief counselor and life coach—reside in Melbourne, Florida, where they share a ministry dedicated to helping people rediscover joy after a life-changing loss. Visit johnfbaggett.com.